The Way of Love

50 Day Bible Challenge

© 2019 Forward Movement

Individual essays are the property of the authors.

All rights reserved.

ISBN: 9780880284806

Printed in USA

Forward
Movement
inspire disciples. empower evangelists.

The Way of Love

50 Day Bible Challenge

Edited by Marek P. Zabriskie

FORWARD MOVEMENT

Cincinnati, Ohio

Foreword

I pray that...Christ may dwell in your hearts through faith, as you are being rooted and grounded in love. I pray that you may have the power to comprehend, with all the saints, what is the breadth and length and height and depth, and to know the love of Christ that surpasses knowledge, so that you may be filled with all the fullness of God.   —Ephesians 3:16-19

Paul's letter to the Ephesians invites us—urges us—to seek to learn and understand the love of Christ, a love that surpasses our earthly comprehension with its width and depth and magnitude. But how can we even begin to grasp this awe-inspiring love? How can we take the first steps on our path to the Way of Love?

The deep roots of our Christian tradition may offer some direction. For centuries, monastic communities have shaped their lives around rhythms and disciplines for following Jesus together. Such a pattern is known as a "Rule of Life." With the help of spiritual leaders across our church, we have pulled together a similar framework for a Rule of Life for the Episcopal branch of the Jesus Movement.

This framework—*The Way of Love*—offers seven spiritual practices for a Jesus-centered life. These practices are: **Turn - Learn - Pray - Worship - Bless - Go - Rest.** How you live out these practices is up to you. They are designed to be both spare and spacious, so that individuals, ministry groups, congregations, and networks can flesh them out in unique ways and build a church-wide treasure trove of stories and resources. There is no specific order you need to follow. If you already keep a Rule or other spiritual disciplines, you might reflect and discover how that path intersects with this one.

Yet with all of its flexibility, the framework still has some core components. Central to each practice is reading and studying God's Holy Word. It's easy to see how Bible study supports the practice of *learn*, but what does the Bible say about *worship*? About *prayer* or *rest*? About *turning* toward God's love or *going* forth in our lives so that we might be a *blessing* toward others? As you might imagine, God has a lot to say! I'm delighted for this offering that can help us better understand each Way of Love practice through the lens of scripture. Over the course of fifty days, a passage from the Bible is paired with a reflection, questions, and a prayer written by faith leaders from across the Episcopal Church. What better path to understanding the glorious love of Christ than through divine scripture?

I am thankful to these faith leaders for sharing their reflections on the Way of Love and to Forward Movement and Bible Challenge editor Marek P. Zabriskie for their commitment to engaging scripture as a critical, life-giving component of the Jesus Movement.

Turn - Learn - Pray - Worship - Bless - Go – Rest. As we enter into reflection, discernment, and commitment around these practices, I pray we will grow as communities that follow the loving, liberating, life-giving way of Jesus. His way has the power to change each of our lives and to change this world.

The Most Rev. Michael B. Curry
XXVII Presiding Bishop
The Episcopal Church

Getting Started

Welcome to The Way of Love Bible Challenge. We are delighted that you are interested in learning more about the practices of the Way of Love through the lens of scripture. Here are some suggestions to consider as you get started:

- You can begin The Way of Love Bible Challenge at any time of year. You can also begin with any practice. They are not in a particular order, so feel free to start with whichever practice is speaking to you. That's why the practices in this book are numbered days one through seven for each week, instead of days one through fifty. Because of the nature of the practices and the Way of Love, any time of year is appropriate for this Bible Challenge, from the fifty days of Eastertide to the summer or fall, or throughout Advent or Lent. You decide what works for you!

- Each day has a manageable amount of reading, a meditation, questions for thought or discussion, and a prayer, written by a host of wonderful authors.

- We suggest that you try to read the Bible each day. This is a great spiritual discipline to establish.

- If you need more than fifty days to read and prayerfully consider each passage, we encourage you to move at a pace that best suits you.

- Many Bible Challenge participants also enjoy reading the Bible on an iPad, iPhone, Kindle, or Nook or listening to the Bible on CDs or on a mobile device using Audio.com, faithcomesbyhearing.com, or Pandora radio. Find what works for you.

How to Read the Bible

Because the Bible is holy scripture, read it with a reverent spirit. We advocate a devotional approach to reading the Bible rather than reading it as a purely intellectual or academic exercise.

- Before reading the Bible, take a moment of silence to put yourself in the presence of God. We then invite you to read this prayer written by Archbishop Thomas Cranmer in 1549.

    > Blessed Lord, who has caused all holy scriptures to be written for our learning: Grant us to hear them, read, mark, learn, and inwardly digest them, that we may embrace and ever hold fast the blessed hope of everlasting life, which you have given us in our Savior Jesus Christ; who lives and reigns with you and the Holy Spirit, one God, for ever and ever. *Amen.*

- Consider using the ancient monastic practice of *lectio divina*. In this form of Bible reading, you read the text and then meditate on a portion of it—a verse or two or even a single word. Mull over the words and their meaning. Then offer a prayer to God based on what you have read, how it has made you feel, or what it has caused you to ponder. Listen in silence for God to respond to your prayer.

- We encourage you to read in the morning, if possible, so that your prayerful reading may spiritually enliven the rest of your day. If you cannot read in the morning, read at a time that suits the rhythm of your life.

Have fun and find spiritual peace and the joy that God desires for you in your daily reading.

Sharing the Way of Love Bible Challenge with Others

One way to hold yourself accountable to reading God's Word is to form a group within your church or community. By participating in The Way of Love Bible Challenge together, you can support one another in your reading, discuss the Bible passages, ask questions, and share how God's Word is transforming your life.

- Ask to have a notice printed in your church newsletter that you are starting a group to participate in The Way of Love Bible Challenge. Invite others to join you. Visit the Center for Biblical Studies website (thecenterforbiblicalstudies.org) to see more suggestions about how churches can participate in The Bible Challenge.

- If you form a Bible Challenge group, consider holding a gathering or meal to celebrate your commitment.

- If you do not want to join a group, you may wish to invite a friend or family member (or two) to share The Way of Love Bible Challenge with you.

- After participating in The Way of Love Bible Challenge, you will be more equipped to support and mentor others in reading the Bible.

Next Steps

After completing The Way of Love Bible Challenge, we encourage you to accept the challenge to read the entire Bible in a year. Reading the Bible each day is a great spiritual discipline to establish. The goal of the Center for Biblical Studies is to help you discover God's wisdom and to create a lifelong spiritual practice of daily Bible reading so that God may guide you through each day of your life.

- Forward Movement's website, www.ForwardMovement.org, offers many resources for learning more about the Bible and engaging scripture. This includes several books in the Bible Challenge series, including each of the four gospels and the Book of Acts as well as *The Social Justice Bible Challenge*.

- In addition, you can find a list of resources at www.thecenterforbiblicalstudies.org. The Center for Biblical Studies also offers a Read the Bible in a Year program and reading plans for the New Testament, Psalms, and Proverbs.

- Once you've finished one complete reading of the Bible, start over and do it again. God may speak differently to you in each reading. Follow the example of U.S. President John Adams, who read through the Bible each year during his adult life. We highly advocate this practice.

We are thrilled that you are participating in The Bible Challenge. May God richly bless you as you prayerfully engage the scriptures each day.

The Way of Love

50 Day Bible Challenge

Turn

Mark 2:13-17

[13]Jesus went out again beside the sea; the whole crowd gathered around him, and he taught them. [14]As he was walking along, he saw Levi son of Alphaeus sitting at the tax booth, and he said to him, "Follow me." And he got up and followed him. [15]And as he sat at dinner in Levi's house, many tax collectors and sinners were also sitting with Jesus and his disciples—for there were many who followed him. [16]When the scribes of the Pharisees saw that he was eating with sinners and tax collectors, they said to his disciples, "Why does he eat with tax collectors and sinners?" [17]When Jesus heard this, he said to them, "Those who are well have no need of a physician, but those who are sick; I have come to call not the righteous but sinners."

Reflection

As people of the twenty-first century, we spend much of our lives building a resume of accomplishments and achievements: where we've studied, the jobs we've had, the goals we've achieved. If we work hard enough, we can accomplish anything. We can earn approval, success, even the love of others. And that "resume" can also include the work we do to be good people. We volunteer our time to help others; we advocate for those who are marginalized; we strive to be good examples to those around us.

But Jesus' call is not something we can work toward; it's not something we earn. Levi, a tax collector whose work was based on taking advantage of other people, clearly doesn't "earn" his call. Jesus doesn't require that Levi clean up his life first or prove anything or bring anything. Jesus simply calls, and Levi responds, turning away from his old life and toward Jesus. In that simple call to "follow me," Jesus points to a new way, and Levi begins living his life in response.

Jesus does not wait until we are ready, or prepared, or perfect. He does not call us because of our resume, or accomplishments, or good works, or even our potential. He calls us to turn toward him, and he gives us what we need to do and to be in response to that call. Levi embodies what it means to repent—to change direction when we are going down the wrong path and to turn toward a life of following Jesus. We, too, are called. We may not feel ready, or worthy, or up to the task. But if we respond and turn toward him, Jesus will give us what we need.

The Rev. Dr. Bill Lupfer
Rector
Trinity Church Wall Street
New York City, New York

Questions

We often believe we are "not ready" to respond to God's call, that we're incapable or inexperienced or unworthy. What gets in your way of answering God's call?

Have there been times in your life when you have truly repented and turned away from the wrong path and toward God?

What led you to "turn," and how did you respond to God's call?

Prayer

O God, by whom the meek are guided in judgment, and light rises up in darkness for the godly: Grant us, in all our doubts and uncertainties, the grace to ask what you would have us do, that the Spirit of wisdom may save us from all false choices, and that in your light we may see light, and in your straight path may not stumble; through Jesus Christ our Lord. *Amen.*

—*The Book of Common Prayer,* p. 832

The Way of Love

Psalm 34

1   I will bless the Lord at all times; *
        his praise shall ever be in my mouth.

2   I will glory in the Lord; *
        let the humble hear and rejoice.

3   Proclaim with me the greatness of the Lord; *
        let us exalt his Name together.

4   I sought the Lord, and he answered me *
        and delivered me out of all my terror.

5   Look upon him and be radiant, *
        and let not your faces be ashamed.

6   I called in my affliction and the Lord heard me *
        and saved me from all my troubles.

7   The angel of the Lord encompasses those who fear him, *
        and he will deliver them.

8   Taste and see that the Lord is good; *
        happy are they who trust in him!

9   Fear the Lord, you that are his saints, *
        for those who fear him lack nothing.

10   The young lions lack and suffer hunger, *
        but those who seek the Lord lack nothing that is good.

11   Come, children, and listen to me; *
       I will teach you the fear of the LORD.

12   Who among you loves life *
       and desires long life to enjoy prosperity?

13   Keep your tongue from evil-speaking *
       and your lips from lying words.

14   Turn from evil and do good; *
       seek peace and pursue it.

15   The eyes of the LORD are upon the righteous, *
       and his ears are open to their cry.

16   The face of the LORD is against those who do evil, *
       to root out the remembrance of them from the earth.

17   The righteous cry, and the LORD hears them *
       and delivers them from all their troubles.

18   The LORD is near to the brokenhearted *
       and will save those whose spirits are crushed.

19   Many are the troubles of the righteous, *
       but the LORD will deliver him out of them all.

20   He will keep safe all his bones; *
       not one of them shall be broken.

21   Evil shall slay the wicked, *
       and those who hate the righteous will be punished.

22   The LORD ransoms the life of his servants, *
       and none will be punished who trust in him.

Reflection

There's a stooped, elderly man I've watched for years on the corner of Market Street in downtown San Francisco, among the tourists and shoppers, who hoists a hand-lettered sign announcing that God saves. He paces up and down the sidewalk by the cable-car line scowling, shouting at people, particularly "homosexuals and fornicators and evildoers," and calling them to repent, by which he means that they should admit they are hopelessly wicked and deserve punishment unless they change their ways. I have a sort of strange affection for this man, despite his unhappiness and anger: He is a kind of prophet—a cracked one, like many before him—and he's not alone in misunderstanding what scripture means by repentance.

To repent is to turn. The psalmist sings: *Turn from evil and do good; seek peace and pursue it.* The invitation to repent is a call to turn away from everything that imprisons us—laziness, busyness, nostalgia, self-loathing, greed, blame, fear—and turn toward God, and toward other people, with desire and joy.

Turning and turning and turning again is a life's work. And the good news is that God is to be found at every turn. Repentance means going after good, pressing on, seeking peace: It can never be about being threatened into obedience, or feeling guilty, or acting sorry. *Taste and see that the Lord is good*, promises the psalmist. *Happy are they who trust in him.* When we turn in repentance, seeking joy, we can trust that we will never be let down.

Sara Miles
Author and Social Justice Activist
San Francisco, California

Questions _____

What do you turn away from? What do you turn toward?

How have you experienced repentance as joy?

Prayer _____

O God, who stays near broken hearts and heals our wounded spirits: Turn us ever toward you, that we may press on to behold you in brightness and know you in joy, through Jesus Christ our Lord. *Amen*.

Luke 5:1-11

[1]Once while Jesus was standing beside the lake of Gennesaret, and the crowd was pressing in on him to hear the word of God, [2]he saw two boats there at the shore of the lake; the fishermen had gone out of them and were washing their nets. [3]He got into one of the boats, the one belonging to Simon, and asked him to put out a little way from the shore. Then he sat down and taught the crowds from the boat. [4]When he had finished speaking, he said to Simon, "Put out into the deep water and let down your nets for a catch." [5]Simon answered, "Master, we have worked all night long but have caught nothing. Yet if you say so, I will let down the nets." [6]When they had done this, they caught so many fish that their nets were beginning to break. [7]So they signaled their partners in the other boat to come and help them. And they came and filled both boats, so that they began to sink. [8]But when Simon Peter saw it, he fell down at Jesus' knees, saying, "Go away from me, Lord, for I am a sinful man!" [9]For he and all who were with him were amazed at the catch of fish that they had taken; [10]and so also were James and John, sons of Zebedee, who were partners with Simon. Then Jesus said to Simon, "Do not be afraid; from now on you will be catching people." [11]When they had brought their boats to shore, they left everything and followed him.

Reflection

"They left everything and followed him." This is such a simple statement—a simple, straightforward statement about a handful of ordinary folks who make a choice to stop in their tracks and turn. They could not possibly know that the choice they make will change not only their own lives, in ways too great to imagine, but also the lives of countless people throughout the world for centuries to come.

These fishermen make a choice to turn from all that is clear and familiar and toward the unknown and the unexplored. And they make this decision for one simple, straightforward reason. They choose to turn their lives not because they seek excitement or yearn for adventure but because Jesus calls them to do so. It is certainly not an obvious decision to make. After all, Simon's life is clear and familiar before Jesus steps into his boat. The same is true for his companions. They know what to do, what to expect. They have all experienced smooth sailing as well as choppy waters. This certainly is not the first time they have worked hard with no great catch to show for it. And yet when Jesus comes along, these rough, hard-working fishermen make a choice to turn and follow him.

That choice does not lead to an easy life for any of those earliest followers or for the many who follow in their footsteps. There will be miracles and celebrations but also struggles and sacrifices. Through it all—the unknown and the unexplored—they find Jesus right there with them, through the Spirit, closer than the air they breathe. And they, and countless others since, find that having Jesus present and trusting him is enough. Indeed, it is more than enough.

The Rev. Canon C.K. Robertson
Canon to the Presiding Bishop
Ministry Beyond the Episcopal Church
New York City, New York

Questions _____

When have you heard or sensed Jesus calling you to turn from the clear and familiar to the unknown and unexplored? How did you respond?

What can you say or do when someone you know is truly struggling and feels like God is far away or unconcerned?

What does it mean to turn and trust Jesus more than yourself? What does that look like in day-to-day life?

Prayer _____

O God, you call us to turn, to dare to trust and follow you: In the midst of life's hardships and struggles, fill us, we pray, with a sense of your presence, shield our hearts from fear and confusion, and by the power of your Spirit grant us strength to step out into the unknown, knowing that you are right there with us; all this we ask in the strong name of Jesus, our Savior and friend. *Amen.*

John 1:35-42

[35]The next day John again was standing with two of his disciples, [36]and as he watched Jesus walk by, he exclaimed, "Look, here is the Lamb of God!"

[37]The two disciples heard him say this, and they followed Jesus. [38]When Jesus turned and saw them following, he said to them, "What are you looking for?" They said to him, "Rabbi" (which translated means Teacher), "where are you staying?" [39]He said to them, "Come and see." They came and saw where he was staying, and they remained with him that day. It was about four o'clock in the afternoon. [40]One of the two who heard John speak and followed him was Andrew, Simon Peter's brother. [41]He first found his brother Simon and said to him, "We have found the Messiah" (which is translated Anointed). [42]He brought Simon to Jesus, who looked at him and said, "You are Simon son of John. You are to be called Cephas" (which is translated Peter).

Reflection

One Sunday morning, I asked my youth group if they would be able to leave everything behind and follow Jesus. One said she didn't think she'd be able to leave her parents and her brother and sisters, no matter how irritating they could be. Another said maybe, but how would he know for sure if the person were Jesus? The conversation turned to whether we would be able to identify Jesus. We talked about seeing Jesus in others like the folks with whom we worship, our teachers and classmates, and the homeless children we meet in our service. If we see Jesus in all of these people, precisely whom do we follow?

John knows that he has been sent to prepare a way for Jesus and builds his ministry around that mission. The very ones who become Jesus' followers are two of John's followers. These men have already decided to follow someone, and with the additional information about Jesus, they turn to follow him instead. I imagine this makes John happy.

Like my youth group teens, we must keep looking for Jesus. When we ask ourselves who Jesus might be, we must look in the mirror and at each other. Just as we look for Jesus in others, people are looking for Jesus in us. Each time we turn toward Jesus, we turn away from something or someone we need to leave behind. Simon and Andrew both left their lives as they knew them for something greater. As we turn again and again toward Jesus, we can also turn to Andrew, Simon, John, Mary Magdalene, Dorcas, and other early followers of Jesus to make our lives more like theirs. As we seek transformation in the One who offers salvation to all, we must turn, turn, and turn again.

Miriam Willard McKenney
Development Director
Forward Movement
Cincinnati, Ohio

Questions

What will you turn from today as you turn toward Jesus? What can you turn from in the short term? What can you leave entirely behind to give you more time for Jesus?

How will you turn toward Jesus today? Choose one of the other practices to anchor your turn. Turn toward scripture (Learn). Turn toward prayer (Pray). Turn toward helping others (Go).

Who might you choose to be a model for your discipleship? Consider John the Baptist, the early disciples, women who followed Jesus, or more contemporary saints.

Prayer

Lord Jesus, who traveled with the disciples on the road to Emmaus: Be with us on the way, that we may know you in the scriptures, in the breaking of bread, and in the hearts of all whom we meet. *Amen.*

—*Saint Augustine's Prayer Book*, p. 85

Luke 5:27-39

^{27}After this he went out and saw a tax collector named Levi, sitting at the tax booth; and he said to him, "Follow me." ^{28}And he got up, left everything, and followed him.

^{29}Then Levi gave a great banquet for him in his house; and there was a large crowd of tax collectors and others sitting at the table with them. ^{30}The Pharisees and their scribes were complaining to his disciples, saying, "Why do you eat and drink with tax collectors and sinners?" ^{31}Jesus answered, "Those who are well have no need of a physician, but those who are sick; ^{32}I have come to call not the righteous but sinners to repentance."

^{33}Then they said to him, "John's disciples, like the disciples of the Pharisees, frequently fast and pray, but your disciples eat and drink. ^{34}Jesus said to them, "You cannot make wedding guests fast while the bridegroom is with them, can you? ^{35}The days will come when the bridegroom will be taken away from them, and then they will fast in those days." ^{36}He also told them a parable: "No one tears a piece from a new garment and sews it on an old garment; otherwise the new will be torn, and the piece from the new will not match the old. ^{37}And no one puts new wine into old wineskins; otherwise the new wine will burst the skins and will be spilled, and the skins will be destroyed. ^{38}But new wine must be put into fresh wineskins. ^{39}And no one after drinking old wine desires new wine, but says, 'The old is good.'"

Reflection

As Jesus sits down with a tax collector and his friends for this first of ten meals described in Luke's Gospel, his actions cut against the grain of cultural expectations. Jesus' reputation already precedes him. Other teachers and their disciples are known for frequent fasting and prayer. In stark contrast, this rebel rabbi seems to be ever eating and drinking. What those standing in judgment miss, however, is how Jesus reveals the radical love of God in table fellowship that comes before a change of behavior.

Jesus loves people as they are. He enjoys spending time with them. This doesn't alter the fact the he wants something better for their lives. Transformed lives do follow, but Jesus doesn't need Levi or his friends to change in order to love him. We know that the relationship with Jesus will disrupt everything for this tax collector—and hopefully for some of his friends.

Jesus answers his critics, "Those who are well have no need of a physician, but those who are sick." He adds a zinger, "I have come to call not the righteous but sinners to repentance." Those hearing Luke's Gospel get the dramatic irony that slipped past the ones Jesus addressed—they too are sinners in need of turning back to God. In fact, we all need the Great Physician. This is most true when we judge others and find them unworthy of God's love.

The gospels make the pattern clear that a change of heart and mind *follows* a relationship with Jesus rather than coming first. Our understanding of the ways we need to turn back to God is informed by reading scripture, prayer, worship, and serving in Jesus' name. Reorienting our life toward God is a natural outgrowth of a relationship with Jesus nourished by spiritual practices. We don't get our lives in order and then connect to our triune God. We find the grace to confront the parts of our lives that don't conform to God's will when we pattern our lives in the Way of Love.

The Rev. Canon Frank S. Logue
Canon to the Ordinary
Diocese of Georgia
Savannah, Georgia

Questions

Why might meals have been essential to Jesus' ministry?

How have your spiritual disciplines led to changes in your life, such as how you spend time or money?

How might you be called now to change a part of your life that does not reflect your faith?

Prayer

Most merciful God, whose Son our Savior Jesus Christ came to call sinners to repentance: Pour out the grace of your Spirit as we turn to you that our lives may give you glory, and by your mercy we may obtain everlasting life; through Jesus Christ our Lord. *Amen.*

Jonah 1:1-6

¹Now the word of the LORD came to Jonah son of Amittai, saying, ²"Go at once to Nineveh, that great city, and cry out against it; for their wickedness has come up before me." ³But Jonah set out to flee to Tarshish from the presence of the LORD. He went down to Joppa and found a ship going to Tarshish; so he paid his fare and went on board, to go with them to Tarshish, away from the presence of the LORD.

⁴But the LORD hurled a great wind upon the sea, and such a mighty storm came upon the sea that the ship threatened to break up. ⁵Then the mariners were afraid, and each cried to his god. They threw the cargo that was in the ship into the sea, to lighten it for them. Jonah, meanwhile, had gone down into the hold of the ship and had lain down, and was fast asleep. ⁶The captain came and said to him, "What are you doing sound asleep? Get up, call on your god! Perhaps the god will spare us a thought so that we do not perish."

Reflection

Sometimes the need to turn and follow God's call involves surprise or an abrupt change of insight we associate with great conversion stories, like that of Saint Paul. To turn then is to encounter something completely unexpected, whether or not it is welcome. I suspect however that for most of us, what we have to turn to is not the unexpected but something we have long known yet felt unable to accept.

The prophet Jonah has an extraordinary call from God, but the most striking (and understandable) part of his story is that he knows it but doesn't want it. Jonah finds the turn he has to make, the call to preach to the Ninevites, distasteful, or perhaps just implausible. He has his preconceptions about where his words might be deserved and well-received, and Nineveh—a wicked, pagan center—doesn't fit the bill.

It's not hard to imagine some modern parallels. Jonah was called to share the mercy of God with people whose behavior plainly indicated they didn't deserve to have words wasted on them. Jonah's story goes on; the result is beyond his worst fears. These contemptible people actually listen and receive mercy. No wonder Jonah didn't want to turn—because the people of Nineveh might turn too.

The ways each of us is being called to turn today may be less spectacular but still share features of Jonah's call. It's likely that we know, deep down, how and where we need to stop what we're doing and listen to what God is saying. It's also likely that our avoidance of a turn isn't about its mystery but about our resistance. God will change us. That might sound like a threat, but it's a promise.

The Very Rev. Dr. Andrew McGowan
Dean and President
Berkeley Divinity School at Yale
New Haven, Connecticut

The Way of Love

Questions

Are there people you would prefer did not turn and hear God's call? Who? And why?

When have you known but resisted God's call to turn?

Prayer

Turn us, O God, and lead us where you will. Let us hear your words to us, and let us be the messengers of your good news in the unlikeliest of places. *Amen.*

Psalm 51

1   Have mercy on me, O God, according to your
                    loving-kindness; *
        in your great compassion blot out my offenses.

2   Wash me through and through from my wickedness *
        and cleanse me from my sin.

3   For I know my transgressions, *
        and my sin is ever before me.

4   Against you only have I sinned *
        and done what is evil in your sight.

5   And so you are justified when you speak *
        and upright in your judgment.

6   Indeed, I have been wicked from my birth, *
        a sinner from my mother's womb.

7   For behold, you look for truth deep within me, *
        and will make me understand wisdom secretly.

8   Purge me from my sin, and I shall be pure; *
        wash me, and I shall be clean indeed.

9   Make me hear of joy and gladness, *
        that the body you have broken may rejoice.

10 Hide your face from my sins *
        and blot out all my iniquities.

11   Create in me a clean heart, O God, *
           and renew a right spirit within me.

12   Cast me not away from your presence *
           and take not your holy Spirit from me.

13   Give me the joy of your saving help again *
           and sustain me with your bountiful Spirit.

14   I shall teach your ways to the wicked, *
           and sinners shall return to you.

15   Deliver me from death, O God, *
           and my tongue shall sing of your righteousness,
           O God of my salvation.

16   Open my lips, O Lord, *
           and my mouth shall proclaim your praise.

17   Had you desired it, I would have offered sacrifice, *
           but you take no delight in burnt-offerings.

18   The sacrifice of God is a troubled spirit; *
           a broken and contrite heart, O God, you will not despise.

19   Be favorable and gracious to Zion, *
           and rebuild the walls of Jerusalem.

20   Then you will be pleased with the appointed sacrifices,
       with burnt-offerings and oblations; *
           then shall they offer young bullocks upon your altar.

Reflection

As the penitential psalm appointed for Ash Wednesday services, Psalm 51 speaks to our turning away from the pain of sin and darkness toward the hope of salvation and light, turning from a life of suffering to the direction of God's love.

When I attended my very first Ash Wednesday service, the litany of Psalm 51 brought me at once to tears and joy. In the throes of divorce and recovery from a painful childhood of sexual abuse, I took to heart the eleventh verse, begging God to "renew a right spirit within me." It was a profound moment of turning for me. I had memorized an Oswald Chambers line asking God to "walk on the chaos of my life just now," and years later Eugene Peterson would translate this verse as "God, make a fresh start in me, shape a Genesis week from the chaos of my life."

Framing this psalm in the language of lament and 12-Step recovery is helpful. The twelve steps are clearly defined: admitting we are powerless, coming to believe, making a decision to turn our lives over to the care of God. When someone has a difficult time with a step, they are encouraged to ask God for the "willingness" first.

Turning to God in the midst of my emotional and spiritual abyss meant saying yes to God, believing that somehow, I would be redeemed and restored to a life of joy. I clung to verse thirteen: "Give me the joy of your saving help again and sustain me with your bountiful Spirit." Saying yes to God takes deep courage, and perhaps if we do not have the courage, we might just ask God for the willingness.

Mary Foster Parmer
Creator and Director, Invite Welcome Connect
Beecken Center of the School of Theology, University of the South
Sewanee, Tennessee

The Way of Love

Questions

Name a moment of turning in your journey of faith. Are you willing to share that moment with others?

Is there a wounded place in your life where you've not asked God for healing? Might you turn and simply ask God for the willingness to be healed?

Prayer

Almighty and eternal God, so draw our hearts to thee, so guide our minds, so fill our imaginations, so control our wills, that we may be wholly thine, utterly dedicated unto thee; and then use us, we pray thee, as thou wilt, and always to thy glory and the welfare of thy people; through our Lord and Savior Jesus Christ. *Amen.*

—*The Book of Common Prayer*, p. 832-33

Learn

John 14:15-23

[15]"If you love me, you will keep my commandments. [16]And I will ask the Father, and he will give you another Advocate, to be with you forever. [17]This is the Spirit of truth, whom the world cannot receive, because it neither sees him nor knows him. You know him, because he abides with you, and he will be in you.

[18]"I will not leave you orphaned; I am coming to you. [19]In a little while the world will no longer see me, but you will see me; because I live, you also will live. [20]On that day you will know that I am in my Father, and you in me, and I in you. [21]They who have my commandments and keep them are those who love me; and those who love me will be loved by my Father, and I will love them and reveal myself to them." [22]Judas (not Iscariot) said to him, "Lord, how is it that you will reveal yourself to us, and not to the world?" [23]Jesus answered him, "Those who love me will keep my word, and my Father will love them, and we will come to them and make our home with them.

Reflection

I am in my twenty-fifth year of priesthood in the Episcopal Church and one aspect of ministry continually surprises and astonishes me. It is preaching. Let me explain.

As you know, our church follows a three-year lectionary cycle, creatively called "Years A, B, and C." In Year A we mostly track the Gospel of Matthew; Year B follows Mark, and Year C spends most of its time in Luke's Gospel. The Gospel of John is interspersed throughout all three cycles. The lesson from the Hebrew scriptures and the second lesson from one of the New Testament epistles also follow their own cycles. All of this is designed to give us a general overview of the narrative flow of the Bible as well as introduce us to theological concepts from the breadth of scripture.

But it repeats itself year after year. With twenty-five years of ordained ministry, this means I have been through the lectionary cycle eight times. When I graduated from seminary, I thought it would be exceedingly difficult to come up with preaching ideas on the same texts year after year. I believed the well of creativity and new ideas would certainly dry up in short order, and I would be left with three files in my desk: one for each year of the lectionary cycle and a tired rehashing of themes and sermons that would be painful for all to endure. And while my sermons may be painful for some to endure, it's not because of their continual reuse.

Here's the part that has continually surprised and amazed me. Have you ever reread a passage from scripture—or just about any book, really—and seen something in it that you missed before? Or have you found yourself in different life circumstances and found the passage speaks to you in an entirely new and unexpected way? Have you just gotten older and found you understand the meanings hidden deep in things that you just couldn't see in youth? This can occur with any piece of literature, but it's been my experience that this sort of thing happens most often when we reread Holy Scripture.

And this is one aspect, I believe, of what Jesus meant when he told his disciples about a "Spirit of truth" that would abide with them. It is also emphasized when he says to them, just a little bit later on, that those "who love me will keep my word, and my Father will love them, and we will come to them and make our home with them." The Lord is continually opening up the word to us, and it never gets stale or tired or rehashed. It lives on and on, new and fresh for ears young and old. And endlessly repeatable.

The Rev. Phillip A. Jackson
Vicar
Trinity Church Wall Street
New York City, New York

Questions

Can you think of a passage of scripture in which its meaning opened up for you over time? How did that meaning change?

What has been your experience in living with the lectionary?

Prayer

Come Holy Spirit of Truth, open for us time and again the wonder and clarity of your living word. *Amen.*

Acts 8:26-40

[26]Then an angel of the Lord said to Philip, "Get up and go toward the south to the road that goes down from Jerusalem to Gaza." (This is a wilderness road.) [27]So he got up and went. Now there was an Ethiopian eunuch, a court official of the Candace, queen of the Ethiopians, in charge of her entire treasury. He had come to Jerusalem to worship [28]and was returning home; seated in his chariot, he was reading the prophet Isaiah. [29]Then the Spirit said to Philip, "Go over to this chariot and join it." [30]So Philip ran up to it and heard him reading the prophet Isaiah. He asked, "Do you understand what you are reading?" [31]He replied, "How can I, unless someone guides me?" And he invited Philip to get in and sit beside him. [32]Now the passage of the scripture that he was reading was this: "Like a sheep he was led to the slaughter, and like a lamb silent before its shearer, so he does not open his mouth. [33]In his humiliation justice was denied him. Who can describe his generation? For his life is taken away from the earth." [34]The eunuch asked Philip, "About whom, may I ask you, does the prophet say this, about himself or about someone else?" [35]Then Philip began to speak, and starting with this scripture, he proclaimed to him the good news about Jesus. [36]As they were going along the road, they came to some water; and the eunuch said, "Look, here is water! What is to prevent me from being baptized?" [38]He commanded the chariot to stop, and both of them, Philip and the eunuch, went down into the water, and Philip baptized him. [39]When they came up out of the water, the Spirit of the Lord snatched

Philip away; the eunuch saw him no more, and went on his way rejoicing. [40]But Philip found himself at Azotus, and as he was passing through the region, he proclaimed the good news to all the towns until he came to Caesarea.

Reflection

As sentient beings, we are predisposed to be responsive to our environment, to be aware of what is around us. Optimal development throughout our lifespan occurs when we interact with a resource-rich environment, experiencing tension between safety and risk, competence and not-yet-knowing. In a perfect world, learning is much more than earning good grades at school.

Today's text from Acts has always captured my imagination. It is a template for discipleship and the process of teaching and learning that makes Christians.

The apostle Philip had to get up and go down a dangerous road from Jerusalem to Gaza. He had to run alongside a moving chariot and hoist himself into it. The person Philip met was a social outcast and a seeker. The eunuch had traveled a long distance to Jerusalem to worship in the temple, and there's a very good chance he was turned away. Certainly, as a foreign-born, castrated male he would not have been allowed into the inner court of the temple where heaven and earth meet. He had never known freedom or belonging and yet he longed to know God. It is likely the eunuch was reading from the prophet Isaiah in a state of existential crisis, "How can I [understand what I am reading], unless someone guides me?"

Anglican theology teaches us that we do not long for God at our core but rather God is longing for us at our core. We are never lost or separate from God, even when our lived experience is as bleak as that of the Ethiopian eunuch. As Jesus reminds his early followers, "The kingdom of God is within you!" So, when we acknowledge what we are truly longing for, we tap into the image and voice of God in us, recognizing that the longing in us is a longing to learn and grow. God in us is pulling us into relationship with God. We learn best when we let the passion of the love of God in us lead.

I believe in learning because I have lived it. Learning comes from longing. Learning without longing is just studying. Longing with purpose and blessed with faithful, responsive mentors is discipleship. It is the Way of Love.

Dr. Lisa Kimball
Associate Dean of Lifelong Learning
Virginia Theological Seminary
Alexandria, Virginia

Questions

For what does your spirit long?

How do you learn best? How do you help others learn?

With whom can you share your deepest questions about faith?

Prayer

Creator, I give you thanks for all you are and all you bring to me for my visit within your creation. In Jesus, you place the gospel at the center of the sacred circle, your church, through which all of creation is related. You show us the way to live a generous and compassionate life. Give me your strength to live with respect for my neighbors and commitment to you as I grow in your spirit, for you are God, now and forever. *Amen.*

—Adapted from The Gathering Prayer,
A Disciple's Prayer Book

Philippians 2:1-8

[1]If then there is any encouragement in Christ, any consolation from love, any sharing in the Spirit, any compassion and sympathy, [2]make my joy complete: be of the same mind, having the same love, being in full accord and of one mind. [3]Do nothing from selfish ambition or conceit, but in humility regard others as better than yourselves. [4]Let each of you look not to your own interests, but to the interests of others. [5]Let the same mind be in you that was in Christ Jesus, [6]who, though he was in the form of God, did not regard equality with God as something to be exploited, [7]but emptied himself, taking the form of a slave, being born in human likeness. And being found in human form, [8]he humbled himself and became obedient to the point of death— even death on a cross.

Reflection

In 1995, Joan Osborne released a song called "One of Us." She explored powerful questions, including, "If God had a face, what would it look like?"

As Christians our faith revolves around Jesus, God with a human face. Jesus is God in a human form "just like one of us." Jesus is God incarnate, walking the earth in our human flesh.

I have a theory that each Christian relates best to one of the three members of the Trinity. Some people really understand God, the Cosmic Creator, who birthed the universe. Others feel the Holy Spirit moving, guiding, and setting them spiritually on fire. But most of us are drawn to Jesus, who allows us to see what God would act like if "God had a face" just like one of us.

In his letter to the Philippians, Paul said, "Let the same mind be in you that was in Christ Jesus." This is one of my favorite Bible verses for it is at the heart of the Christian journey. To see the world as Christ sees it, to feel compassion as Christ feels compassion, and to react as Christ would react is to have the same mind in us "that was in Christ Jesus."

Paul says of Jesus, "though he was in the form of God, [Jesus] did not regard equality with God as something to be exploited, but emptied himself, taking the form of a slave, being born in human likeness." The Greek word for this self-emptying is *kenosis*.

A priest friend of mine studied theology in Rome. While in Italy, he purchased a painting depicting Jesus on the cross. The artist painted a cross and then applied a large arc-shaped brushstroke of paint from the top to the bottom of the cross like a body hanging on the cross.

He entitled it *kenosis*, signifying Jesus pouring himself out upon the cross for our sins.

When we "let the same mind be in [us] that was in Christ Jesus" we develop not just our mind but also our heart, soul, and character to see, respond to, and love the world just as Jesus did and does. Developing the mind of Christ comes from engaging scripture, devoting ourselves to prayer, spending time in Christian fellowship, serving those in need, and finding Christ in the eucharist. Developing the mind of Christ stimulates us to a form of self-emptying so that the love and grace of God pour through us and into the lives of others.

The Rev. Marek P. Zabriskie
Founder, The Bible Challenge
Rector, Christ Church
Greenwich, Connecticut

Questions

What spiritual practices do you engage in that allow you to develop the mind of Christ? Have you ever tried scripture memorization?

Do you engage scripture four or more times a week? Studies reveal that this is the best way to grow spiritually and develop the mind of Christ.

Prayer

Gracious God, help us to learn the mind of Christ that we might allow your Spirit to pour through us and into the lives of others. Help us to empty ourselves in order that your holy, life-giving Spirit might fill and transform us. *Amen.*

Philippians 4:4-9

[4]Rejoice in the Lord always; again I will say, Rejoice. [5]Let your gentleness be known to everyone. The Lord is near. [6]Do not worry about anything, but in everything by prayer and supplication with thanksgiving let your requests be made known to God. [7]And the peace of God, which surpasses all understanding, will guard your hearts and your minds in Christ Jesus.

[8]Finally, beloved, whatever is true, whatever is honorable, whatever is just, whatever is pure, whatever is pleasing, whatever is commendable, if there is any excellence and if there is anything worthy of praise, think about these things. [9]Keep on doing the things that you have learned and received and heard and seen in me, and the God of peace will be with you.

Reflection

On a tour of the Tower of London, I saw the cell behind the dining area of the main house where special prisoners were kept. The learned prisoners were literally in the sight of the official, by proximity. It makes you wonder what could be written from a place like that. Consider Paul, who is writing from jail to the Philippians. What could Paul know about freedom when he is literally in prison? What is a good thing, a right action? What is rejoicing in confinement? Maybe the questions we should be asking are about the ways in which we are confined and imprisoned, even if (and when) we are in the house of the powerful.

A friend who taught theology in a seminary and occasionally in a state penitentiary said that the people in prison understood Paul in a completely different way. When the discussion of freedom is not metaphorical but literal, the words mean something else. In prison (and perhaps in life), one of the few things we can control is our own minds, our thinking. This great spiritual insight is a simple truth in jail. Those of us who are not imprisoned often feel free to resist truths like this, bound as we are by busyness, consumerism, and self-doubt.

I learned these verses as a child, in a song: "Rejoice in the Lord always, and again I say rejoice." We learned it as a round, a delightful, simple tune to have in the potential earworm file. Simple and yet a necessary rebuke to my days of worry and frustration at the small and large obstacles of living. And so as the pain of the world threatens to chase the hope of Christ from our sight, we are invited to remember and relearn the good, the righteous, the holy, and the simple—and rejoice.

The Rev. Winnie Varghese
Director of Justice and Reconciliation
Trinity Church Wall Street
New York City, New York

Questions

What are the barriers to joy in your life? What do you associate with "whatever is true, whatever is honorable, whatever is just, whatever is pure, whatever is pleasing, whatever is commendable?"

Prison is a political reality that points to more than crime and punishment. Civil rights lawyer Michelle Alexander highlights the racial disparities in our criminal justice system and their connection to our nation's heritage of slavery. How is this manifest in your community?

Prayer

Accept, O Lord, our thanks and praise for all that you have done for us. We thank you for the splendor of the whole creation, for the beauty of this world, for the wonder of life, and for the mystery of love. We thank you for the blessing of family and friends, and for the loving care which surrounds us on every side. We thank you for setting us at tasks which demand our best efforts, and for leading us to accomplishments which satisfy and delight us. We thank you also for those disappointments and failures that lead us to acknowledge our dependence on you alone. Above all, we thank you for your Son Jesus Christ; for the truth of his Word and the example of his life; for his steadfast obedience, by which he overcame temptation; for his dying, through which he overcame death; and for his rising to life again, in which we are raised to the life of your kingdom. Grant us the gift of your Spirit, that we may know him and make him known; and through him, at all times and in all places, may give thanks to you in all things. *Amen.*

—The Book of Common Prayer, p. 836

Matthew 7:24-29

[24]"Everyone then who hears these words of mine and acts on them will be like a wise man who built his house on rock. [25]The rain fell, the floods came, and the winds blew and beat on that house, but it did not fall, because it had been founded on rock. [26]And everyone who hears these words of mine and does not act on them will be like a foolish man who built his house on sand. [27]The rain fell, and the floods came, and the winds blew and beat against that house, and it fell—and great was its fall!" [28]Now when Jesus had finished saying these things, the crowds were astounded at his teaching, [29]for he taught them as one having authority, and not as their scribes.

Reflection

Hear and act. Listen and learn.

It seems so easy! But how many times have you experienced when someone—perhaps even yourself—heard wise instructions and did nothing or, worse, the exact opposite. It makes little sense, and yet time and again a familiar refrain resounds: "Ah, but I know better."

It is the sin of Eden, the old proverbial pride that blinds us from truly learning those things that can help and perhaps even save us. We insist on doing things our way, pursuing short cuts and sure things instead of listening and learning, hearing and acting on what we have heard.

I am reminded of the story of a seeker who traveled the world in search of the key to life. His search led him to the top of a great mountain where he found a revered teacher who could impart to him the treasure he so eagerly sought. Upon welcoming the seeker into his humble dwelling and hearing why he was there, the teacher bid him to sit and began to pour a cup of tea.

While pouring the tea, the teacher prattled on incessantly about the mountain, the weather, anything other than the thing for which the seeker had traveled so long and hard to hear from him. The seeker tried to sit dutifully and not interrupt. But as he watched, the teacher continued to talk and pour until the tea filled the cup and flowed over into the saucer and then onto the table and the floor. "Stop!" the seeker blurted out. "Can you not see that the cup is full! There's no room for any more!"

The teacher stopped and smiled. "Yes, and even so, you are so full of your own preconceptions and opinions and certainties that there is no room for anything else. Before I can give you the treasure you seek, you must first empty your cup."

Jesus has much to share with you and me today. But perhaps we must empty our cups.

The Rev. Canon C. K. Robertson
Canon to the Presiding Bishop
Ministry Beyond the Episcopal Church
New York City, New York

Questions

What are some of the things that block you from truly learning from Jesus? What can you do about them?

Amidst the struggles and divisions we face in our time, what are some practical things we can learn from Jesus' sayings and stories in the gospels that could bring real and lasting change to us and the world around us?

How is wisdom different from knowledge?

Who are some people you know who are truly wise and from whom you could learn?

Prayer

God of all wisdom and understanding, you share with all who would listen the way of love, the way of life: Give us grace to lay aside our own preconceptions and certainties, and by your Spirit help us to be open to fresh insights and learnings that ultimately come from you; in the Name of Jesus, our teacher and guide. *Amen.*

Psalm 1

1   Happy are they who have not walked in the counsel of
the wicked, *
      nor lingered in the way of sinners,
      nor sat in the seats of the scornful!

2   Their delight is in the law of the LORD, *
      and they meditate on his law day and night.

3   They are like trees planted by streams of water,
bearing fruit in due season, with leaves that do not wither; *
      everything they do shall prosper.

4   It is not so with the wicked; *
      they are like chaff which the wind blows away.

5   Therefore the wicked shall not stand upright when
judgment comes, *
      nor the sinner in the council of the righteous.

6   For the LORD knows the way of the righteous, *
      but the way of the wicked is doomed.

Reflection

In the early hours of August 26, 2017, my family was hunkered down in our home near Houston, Texas, and petrified with fear. Hurricane Harvey had exploded from a tropical depression to a major hurricane in about forty hours, and we were experiencing some of the worst of the storm, with one tornado warning after another. My wife was in the hall bathroom with our daughter, Riley, and Scout, the cockapoo. I was in the hall closet. Through a crack in the door, I could see that the storm was raging—wicked and angry.

Both my wife and I were calling out words from prayers we knew by heart, Bible verses that brought us consolation and eased our fear. Other than a few branches and a shingle or two, the storm passed over our home causing little physical damage. That being said, it was the longest and most frightening night of our lives.

Our world is experiencing a different kind of storm. It is a time of grave and wicked darkness. Relationships are strained and broken. Hatred is spewed forth from all sides. We find it hard to love—not to mention, trust—our neighbors. We are on a small boat, and the storm is raging all around us. We toss and turn and are fearful that the boat might sink.

And then…we call out the name of the one who is Love. We read the stories and sing the hymns that glorify God's name. We meditate on these words day and night. We gather in community, and little by little, darkness turns to light. The winds begin to settle. The fear begins to ease. Love has overcome wickedness.

Roger Hutchison
Director of Christian Formation and Parish Life
Palmer Memorial Episcopal Church
Houston, Texas

Question

Do you read the scriptures on a daily basis or do you turn to them only in times of need, when you are fearful or anxious?

Reflect on a time when, gathered in community, you felt the presence of God's love.

Prayer

O God, you have bound us together in a common life. Help us, in the midst of our struggles for justice and truth, to confront one another without hatred or bitterness, and to work together with mutual forbearance and respect; through Jesus Christ our Lord. *Amen.*

—*The Book of Common Prayer*, p. 824

Micah 4:1-5

¹In days to come the mountain of the LORD's house shall be established as the highest of the mountains, and shall be raised up above the hills. Peoples shall stream to it, ²and many nations shall come and say: "Come, let us go up to the mountain of the LORD, to the house of the God of Jacob; that he may teach us his ways and that we may walk in his paths." For out of Zion shall go forth instruction, and the word of the LORD from Jerusalem. ³He shall judge between many peoples, and shall arbitrate between strong nations far away; they shall beat their swords into plowshares, and their spears into pruning hooks; nation shall not lift up sword against nation, neither shall they learn war any more; ⁴but they shall all sit under their own vines and under their own fig trees, and no one shall make them afraid; for the mouth of the LORD of hosts has spoken.

⁵For all the peoples walk, each in the name of its god, but we will walk in the name of the LORD our God forever and ever.

Reflection

Beating our swords into plowshares has been a long-promised outcome of life in Christ. One day, the peaceable kingdom will return, and we will have no need for war and strife. We will live in harmony and peace. It's a nice idea; it sounds sweet, like something you might hear in Sunday School as a child. I wonder though: Have you ever considered that it might be a real opportunity?

The word "learn" jumps out at me in this passage. The prophet Micah declares that nations will not "learn war any more." For most of my life I have considered violence and war a kind of default of humanity. Either through our inherit sinful nature or our base desire for destruction, humans are wired for destruction and death. Micah makes it clear that war is a learned process.

My stepfather's memory is fading, but he still recalls basic training, his time in Vietnam, and his life as a drill instructor for the 82nd Airborne. When I talked with him about the concept of "learning war," he gave an uncomfortable laugh. Sure, he said, people might be capable of violence but not capable of war without some kind of training. War is too big. War is too gruesome without some unifying structure for individuals to come together and make war as one nation. Given this idea of learning war, I wonder what it would look like if we learned (and practiced) discipleship with as much fervor and urgency as we do in learning war. In Micah's text, we see a vision for a place where all violent notions fall away like rolling water. With no need to worry about nation versus nation, we are left with the ability to focus on the bounty of God's abundance.

Bill Campbell
Executive Director
Forma
Alexandria, Virginia

Questions

What are you doing to turn your swords into plowshares?

What are you doing to no longer learn war?

Prayer

God, in the moment of the world's creation, you called everything into being and said that it was very good. Help us to see that all that we need to glorify you and your son Jesus is here in this very good world. Help us to see that we are all one nation before you, that we all belong to your kingdom. Help us to see that Zion is not far off, that you are here with us. Be with us now and in our time of need and guide us into your peace. *Amen*.

Pray

Luke 11:1-13

[1]He was praying in a certain place, and after he had finished, one of his disciples said to him, "Lord, teach us to pray, as John taught his disciples." [2]He said to them, "When you pray, say: Father, hallowed be your name. Your kingdom come. [3]Give us each day our daily bread. [4]And forgive us our sins, for we ourselves forgive everyone indebted to us. And do not bring us to the time of trial." [5]And he said to them, "Suppose one of you has a friend, and you go to him at midnight and say to him, 'Friend, lend me three loaves of bread; [6]for a friend of mine has arrived, and I have nothing to set before him.' [7]And he answers from within, 'Do not bother me; the door has already been locked, and my children are with me in bed; I cannot get up and give you anything.' [8]I tell you, even though he will not get up and give him anything because he is his friend, at least because of his persistence he will get up and give him whatever he needs. [9]"So I say to you, Ask, and it will be given you; search, and you will find; knock, and the door will be opened for you. [10]For everyone who asks receives, and everyone who searches finds, and for everyone who knocks, the door will be opened. [11]Is there anyone among you who, if your child asks for a fish, will give a snake instead of a fish? [12]Or if the child asks for an egg, will give a scorpion? [13]If you then, who are evil, know how to give good gifts to your children, how much more will the heavenly Father give the Holy Spirit to those who ask him!"

Reflection

Never miss a chance to take a pilgrimage to the Holy Land. While visiting some site during your pilgrimage, you will find yourself saying, "I thought that I believed, but now I *really* believe," and your faith will come alive in a breathtaking new way.

It may happen while touching the Wailing Wall, while standing on the Mount of Beatitudes, or while visiting the Church of the Pater Noster located on the Mount of Olives. This church was built over a cave where Jesus is reported to have frequently gone to pray to God in solitude. Inside the church, the Lord's Prayer (*Pater Noster* in Latin) is written in 123 different languages.

Jesus was devoted to prayer. He prayed before each major act of ministry. He prayed before calling his disciples and for forty days and nights before being tempted by the devil.

Jesus prayed before and after giving the Sermon on the Mount and before multiplying the fish and loaves and feeding the five thousand. He prayed before entering Jerusalem on his final visit. Jesus prayed at the Last Supper, before being crucified, and while hanging on the cross.

Prayer was integral to Jesus' life. The disciples realized that there was a direct connection between Jesus' focus on prayer and his amazing power to heal, teach, preach, and perform miracles. So, they asked him, "Lord, teach us to pray."

Jesus responded by teaching them the Lord's Prayer. It is not a magical prayer but serves as a model for all prayers. Perhaps the most crucial phrase is "thy kingdom come, thy will be done." When we unite our will with God's will, we experience union with God and miracles occur.

Study the life of any great saint and you will discover someone powerfully steeped in prayer. No wonder Francis Thompson, author of the *The Hound of Heaven*, described prayer as the "sword of the saints."

The Rev. Marek P. Zabriskie
Founder, The Bible Challenge
Rector, Christ Church
Greenwich, Connecticut

Questions

What keeps you from being more devoted and regular in prayer?

Are you often too busy to pray? Has it ever occurred to you that when you are too busy to pray, you are most in need of prayer?

Do you think that prayer is more about listening or about speaking?

Silence is often called the language that God speaks. How comfortable are you with this type of "conversation?"

Prayer

O Lord, you know our every thought, need, worry, hurt, loss, dream, hope, and fear before we even open our lips to utter a prayer. Help us to turn to you, the ultimate partner, for wisdom, strength, comfort, healing, inspiration, love, forgiveness, guidance, and grace. You are available to us at all times and in all places, and you know the solution to our problem before we are even aware that we face a challenge. Fill us with your Holy Spirit that we might bear the beams of your love to all whom we meet. *Amen*.

Mark 13:14-22

[14]"But when you see the desolating sacrilege set up where it ought not to be (let the reader understand), then those in Judea must flee to the mountains; [15]the one on the housetop must not go down or enter the house to take anything away; [16]the one in the field must not turn back to get a coat. [17]Woe to those who are pregnant and to those who are nursing infants in those days! [18]Pray that it may not be in winter. [19]For in those days there will be suffering, such as has not been from the beginning of the creation that God created until now, no, and never will be. [20]And if the Lord had not cut short those days, no one would be saved; but for the sake of the elect, whom he chose, he has cut short those days. [21]And if anyone says to you at that time, 'Look! Here is the Messiah!' or 'Look! There he is!'—do not believe it. [22]False messiahs and false prophets will appear and produce signs and omens, to lead astray, if possible, the elect.

Reflection

In graphic terms, Jesus foretells the devastation of the last days—there won't even be time to run back to the house and get your coat! Not even the joy of bringing a child into the world will mitigate the terror of it; your new parenthood will only add to your fear.

Pray that it may not be in winter, he says. You and I know all about that kind of prayer. It's the one you breathe while waiting for the ambulance to come in the middle of the night. The one you say when there are layoffs and you've been asked to report to the personnel office tomorrow morning. It's the prayer you say after your wife has told you she thinks maybe the two of you should separate for a while. It is this prayer: *Please, please, please—don't let it get even worse than it already is.*

Is there anything that can deliver us from our terror? Certainly it is not the case that people of prayer are spared tragedy in their lives. It comes to all of us. But it *is* true that the life of prayer can prepare us for it. Christ is not present with us only in the good times. Your moment closest to Christ is not always that time when everything worked out perfectly for you. It might turn out to be that moment when *nothing* did, that time when you found yourself at the very end of your rope, with nowhere left to turn.

Maybe you didn't know that Jesus was there with you until it was over. Maybe it took you a while to know that you couldn't have survived it without him. Maybe you saw that prayer was not an end run around the sorrows of life but the way to walk through them, side by side with the One who will never leave you.

The Rev. Barbara Cawthorne Crafton
Episcopal Priest and Author
Boulder, Colorado

Questions

Think of the last several weeks. What has been your moment closest to Christ? Was it a happy moment or a difficult one? Did you know he was there at the time, or did this understanding dawn on you only later on?

Think of a time when Christ seemed absent—your moment farthest from Christ. Looking back at it now, how do you see it? What did you need? What did you have?

Think of a time when you prayed *desperately*. What words did you use in your prayer?

Prayer

Be present with me, Lord Jesus, in this my time of great need. Help me to see you more clearly than I do right now and to remember the times when I have seen you in my life. You have been my God throughout my life, in good times and bad; give me the peace that comes from knowing you are here and will never leave me. *Amen.*

Psalm 62:5-9

5   They bless with their lips, *
        but in their hearts they curse.

6   For God alone my soul in silence waits; *
        truly, my hope is in him.

7   He alone is my rock and my salvation, *
        my stronghold, so that I shall not be shaken.

8   In God is my safety and my honor; *
        God is my strong rock and my refuge.

9   Put your trust in him always, O people, *
        pour out your hearts before him, for God is our refuge.

Reflection

Put "prayer" into an online bookseller search box, and you'll find books about prayer techniques for improving your finances, getting the answers you want, even ones guaranteeing success. In other words, the books pretend to offer ways to control God. Talk about hubris! Fortunately there are also books written by people who choose humility, honesty, and true reverence—people who understand that prayer is about sacred relationship initiated by God.

These verses from Psalm 62 point us to a relationship rooted in trust and vulnerability. We are encouraged to pour out our hearts. This is not the type of pouring out we do on social media, with carefully constructed images designed to cast us in the best light. In prayer, the image we present is irrelevant, because God, who invites us to pour out everything—good, bad, and in-between—already knows. God welcomes our confidences with understanding, tenderness, and forgiveness. God offers grace and the clarity of vision we need to grow in compassionate, generous loving that faintly echoes God's own. As the psalmist proclaims, God is our rock, our fortress, our deliverance, our refuge. These symbols engender trust, emboldening us to ask God to lift us out of destructive traps of ego, resentment, and efforts to control. Leaning into that trust leads to life lived in wonder and gratitude. As we allow ourselves to be immersed in such wonder, words will drift away. The outpouring of needs, fears, hurts, self-pity, and even our most joyous gratitude will slow to a trickle. We will find that silence enfolds and fills us. We will rediscover what it means that "for God alone my soul in silence waits." We will receive the sort of prayer that no book can describe, that only trust can receive.

The Rev. Sr. Diana Dorothea Doncaster, CT
Sister and Priest
Community of the Transfiguration
Glendale, Ohio

Questions _____

Are there parts of you or topics that, in your prayers and worship, you try to avoid? What is it that keeps you from pouring your heart out about them?

Have you ever tried to control or bargain with God? What circumstances led you in that direction?

Prayer _____

Living God, do you truly listen when I pour out my heart? Help me to trust you in the midst of doubt, to sit silently with you even when you seem absent. Help me to risk trusting that you are truly my salvation and refuge no matter what happens. *Amen*.

1 Kings 19:1-12

[1]Ahab told Jezebel all that Elijah had done, and how he had killed all the prophets with the sword. [2]Then Jezebel sent a messenger to Elijah, saying, "So may the gods do to me, and more also, if I do not make your life like the life of one of them by this time tomorrow." [3]Then he was afraid; he got up and fled for his life, and came to Beersheba, which belongs to Judah; he left his servant there.

[4]But he himself went a day's journey into the wilderness, and came and sat down under a solitary broom tree. He asked that he might die: "It is enough; now, O Lord, take away my life, for I am no better than my ancestors." [5]Then he lay down under the broom tree and fell asleep. Suddenly an angel touched him and said to him, "Get up and eat." [6]He looked, and there at his head was a cake baked on hot stones, and a jar of water. He ate and drank, and lay down again. [7]The angel of the Lord came a second time, touched him, and said, "Get up and eat, otherwise the journey will be too much for you." [8]He got up, and ate and drank; then he went in the strength of that food forty days and forty nights to Horeb the mount of God. [9]At that place he came to a cave, and spent the night there. Then the word of the Lord came to him, saying, "What are you doing here, Elijah?" [10]He answered, "I have been very zealous for the Lord, the God of hosts; for the Israelites have forsaken your covenant, thrown down your altars, and killed your prophets with the sword. I alone am left, and they are seeking my life, to take it away."

[11]He said, "Go out and stand on the mountain before the Lord,

The Way of Love

for the LORD is about to pass by." Now there was a great wind, so strong that it was splitting mountains and breaking rocks in pieces before the LORD, but the LORD was not in the wind; and after the wind an earthquake, but the LORD was not in the earthquake; [12]and after the earthquake a fire, but the LORD was not in the fire; and after the fire a sound of sheer silence.

Reflection

The first time God descended on Horeb/Sinai was when Moses received the commandments written on stone tablets. Then, the thunder and lightning offered a declarative sign of God's presence. But in Elijah's story the tempest is just wild weather. Bread for the journey, which the angel initially provides, or the earth-shaking storm are the conventional places Elijah expects to find God. Yet God by nature tends toward the unconventional places, since new revelation gets our attention precisely by breaking through our concentric circles of normalcy and expectation. God is revealed to Elijah in the aftermath, in the "sound of sheer silence," or as another familiar translation puts it: in a "still small voice."

Prayer is often conventionally taught and practiced as the way we talk to God. This is a good start, but it's only the first half of the conversation. Spiritual communities where prayer is practiced as central to the individual and common life usually describe prayer as more about listening than speaking. At times silence may be perceived as divine absence, but with regular practice, listening prayer begins to open our field of perception. We learn to listen through the chatter of our minds, tuning our awareness to a presence in and through all things.

Listening prayer is not only inward but outward-directed as well. As we increasingly sense God in the still, small, and subtle, we inevitably discover God in the peripheral and marginalized and edgy. Watch what happens next when Elijah listens in silence: His prophetic courage and message come blazing back in spades!

"Absolutely unmixed attention is prayer," said philosopher Simone Weil. Some form of contemplative awareness is increasingly taught by spiritual teachers from many traditions as a central pillar in our collective work of facing global cultural and spiritual challenges. Begin a practice of simple noticing, even if for just a few minutes each day, and watch where it takes you!

The Rev. Daniel Simons
Director of Spiritual Formation
Trinity Retreat Center
West Cornwall, Connecticut

Questions

Take an inventory of your existing daily and weekly rituals. Which ones bring you closer to God and your true self? How might these routines become opportunities to listen more fully? And what additional practice calls you to go even deeper?

Take a walk in nature until your attention is captured by a particular item or event. Stop and notice everything about that one thing in ever greater and smaller detail for several minutes. What do you notice about the overall experience? What do you "hear?"

Prayer

O God, yours is the silence of presence, encompassing and filling all things, as close to us as our very breath; give us courageous hearts to listen into that great silence, to hear your voice as it speaks within, calls us by our true name, and sends us on our truth path. We pray this in Christ, who is bringing all creation to its fullness. *Amen.*

1 Samuel 3:1-10

¹Now the boy Samuel was ministering to the LORD under Eli. The word of the Lord was rare in those days; visions were not widespread.

²At that time Eli, whose eyesight had begun to grow dim so that he could not see, was lying down in his room; ³the lamp of God had not yet gone out, and Samuel was lying down in the temple of the LORD, where the ark of God was. ⁴Then the LORD called, "Samuel! Samuel!" and he said, "Here I am!" ⁵and ran to Eli, and said, "Here I am, for you called me." But he said, "I did not call; lie down again." So he went and lay down. ⁶The LORD called again, "Samuel!" Samuel got up and went to Eli, and said, "Here I am, for you called me." But he said, "I did not call, my son; lie down again." ⁷Now Samuel did not yet know the LORD, and the word of the LORD had not yet been revealed to him. ⁸The LORD called Samuel again, a third time. And he got up and went to Eli, and said, "Here I am, for you called me." Then Eli perceived that the LORD was calling the boy. ⁹Therefore Eli said to Samuel, "Go, lie down; and if he calls you, you shall say, 'Speak, LORD, for your servant is listening.'" So Samuel went and lay down in his place.

¹⁰Now the LORD came and stood there, calling as before, "Samuel! Samuel!" And Samuel said, "Speak, for your servant is listening."

Reflection

Little did Samuel know that saying, "Speak, Lord, for your servant is listening," would lead to his vocation as priest, prophet, and judge of Israel. As followers of Jesus, we all have a common vocation to love God. God speaks to everyone, whether we realize it or not. We don't have to be religious experts or experience a dramatic act. Samuel was a boy minding his own business until God called his name.

Part of our life's work is to create an atmosphere conducive to hearing the voice of God, revealing and leading us to our individual expression of our common call to love God. Samuel's call was discerned with the help of Eli and for the benefit of his people. Samuel learned that hearing God at times meant that he must speak a prophetic word, a hard truth, because he loved God and loved God's people. This is true for us today and part of the reason why we each need to participate in communities of faith that support mutual discernment and help us to be a prophetic presence in the world.

Lying down in the quiet of the temple, in the presence of God, taking their rest from work, Eli and Samuel let the sounds and cares of the day recede. Having times of rest and leaving space for God to speak to us as we pray nurtures our awareness of our connectedness to God and one another. God speaks to us through scripture, worship, relationships, sabbath, and particularly through prayer.

It is easy to lose sight of our spiritual path and forget the sound of God's voice. Be assured that God is always seeking to keep our eyes and ears attuned to God's vision of justice and love and the part we each play in making God's beloved community grow and flourish.

The Rev. Dr. Shannon MacVean-Brown
Interim Rector, St. Thomas Church
Franklin, Indiana

The Way of Love

Questions

Theologian Frederick Buechner says, "The place God calls you to is the place where your deep gladness and the world's deep hunger meet." As you pray, take a piece of paper and draw a line down the center. On the left side, write, "What gives me joy?" On the right, put this question: "What needs of the world affect me?" On the other side of the paper draw a line down the center and on the left, write, "What am I currently doing in ministry?" On the right side, ask this question: "What ministry would I like to explore?" Let the questions sit with you for a while, then begin to write your responses. You may want to spread this inventory out over a couple of days or weeks.

Pray with these words and concerns for a month. Listen for what God is saying to you about what you are called to do. Perhaps you will hear confirmation that you are connecting to your call. Maybe you will hear the possibility of a new ministry opportunity or the urging to discontinue something you are doing to make time for something new. What are you hearing God say to you?

Prayer

God of immeasurable love, thank you for calling each one of us by name. In our common call to love you, may the Holy Spirit guide us in creating discerning communities of faith. Open our ears to your voice and may our eyes hold fast to your vision of a church that prophetically embodies your love in the world, as modeled by your Son our Savior Jesus Christ. *Amen.*

Luke 18:1-8

[1]Then Jesus told them a parable about their need to pray always and not to lose heart. [2]He said, "In a certain city there was a judge who neither feared God nor had respect for people. [3]In that city there was a widow who kept coming to him and saying, 'Grant me justice against my opponent.' [4]For a while he refused; but later he said to himself, 'Though I have no fear of God and no respect for anyone, [5]yet because this widow keeps bothering me, I will grant her justice, so that she may not wear me out by continually coming.'" [6]And the Lord said, "Listen to what the unjust judge says. [7]And will not God grant justice to his chosen ones who cry to him day and night? Will he delay long in helping them? [8]I tell you, he will quickly grant justice to them. And yet, when the Son of Man comes, will he find faith on earth?"

Reflection

I love that Jesus felt this parable was perfect to teach his disciples to pray always and not lose heart. The widow is incessant in her insistence, and the judge, whom Jesus calls unjust, is just fed up.

Prayer sometimes feels like that to me. I beg God to hear me over and over and am faced with conflicting messages from well-meaning people: "Leave your prayer at the altar or at God's feet and let God take care of it," they say. "You don't have enough faith if you keep asking," others say. I say, "When I truly want or need something, I will ask several times until it is done." I agree with the acronym PUSH: Pray Until Something Happens. It may seem silly, but it is basically what Jesus tells his disciples.

This passage says we should pray always. When I was a teenager, a mentor, Chayanne, helped me learn to pray all the time. No, I do not stop and say, "The Lord be with you." No, I do not close my eyes and bow my head—especially when I am driving! No, I do not get on my knees. What Chayanne taught me was to pray silently or aloud constantly about everything anywhere. As I type this, I am praying for you and for the words being typed. I pray short, usually silent, quick messages—prayer texts, of sorts—throughout the day. *Please help me get there on time. Thank you for my family. Please let my car make it to the nearest gas station.* God listens and knows my heart, so a one-word prayer is always appropriate: *No! HELP! Yeah! Thanks! Love! BRB!*

No matter what you've heard or been told, Jesus says: Keep asking, keep praying, don't lose heart.

Dr. Sandra T. Montes
Spanish Ministry Consultant and Musician
Sugar Land, Texas

Questions

What text or prayer will you send Jesus at this very moment?

Is there anything for which you need to pray always and not lose heart?

Prayer

Dear Jesus, help us to be incessant in prayer and just in our dealings. Thank you for listening and for answering our prayers. Teach us to pray when we feel we can't and remind us you can always be reached. En tu nombre. *Amén.*

Jonah 2:1-9

[1]Then Jonah prayed to the LORD his God from the belly of the fish, [2]saying, "I called to the LORD out of my distress, and he answered me; out of the belly of Sheol I cried, and you heard my voice. [3]You cast me into the deep, into the heart of the seas, and the flood surrounded me; all your waves and your billows passed over me. [4]Then I said, 'I am driven away from your sight; how shall I look again upon your holy temple?' [5]The waters closed in over me; the deep surrounded me; weeds were wrapped around my head [6]at the roots of the mountains. I went down to the land whose bars closed upon me forever; yet you brought up my life from the Pit, O LORD my God. [7]As my life was ebbing away, I remembered the LORD; and my prayer came to you, into your holy temple. [8]Those who worship vain idols forsake their true loyalty. [9]But I with the voice of thanksgiving will sacrifice to you; what I have vowed I will pay. Deliverance belongs to the LORD!"

Reflection

The Assyrians have laid waste to the Kingdom of Israel, carrying ten of the twelve tribes into captivity. Yet God calls Jonah to preach repentance in the capitol of the empire. The prophet frets that he might succeed—he would prefer to see the great city in an ash heap. Wouldn't it be just like God to forgive *them*?! Jonah is on the run from God when a storm threatens the boat. Jonah tells the mariners to cast him into the sea. The sea above calms as deep beneath the waves, Jonah is swallowed whole. The prophet calls out to God in this prayer from the belly of a great fish. Jonah says, "he answered me" and "you heard my voice" and responds in gratitude to God at being rescued in the unlikeliest manner. Jonah ends his prayer with the passage at the center of this 48-verse book, "Deliverance belongs to the Lord." Jonah is right. Who God rescues is God's business. Even so, the prophet wants to limit God's mercy. Jonah crosses Nineveh, crying out, "Forty days more and Nineveh shall be overthrown." Soon everyone from the king in the palace to a donkey in a stall is fasting from food and drink while covered in ashes as a sign of repentance. God relents from punishment yet stays with Jonah in his anger at the grace extended to Nineveh.

Like Jonah, I want prayer to be a conduit for getting wishes granted. This is not how prayer works. Prayer maintains the connection in an ongoing relationship through which God transforms our hearts and minds. Like Jonah, I find God remains true to God's own self, while prayer changes me. This happens not when we name our demands, telling God when and how to act. Instead, we are to listen as well as speak. God hears us—and speaks best in silence.

The Rev. Canon Frank S. Logue
Canon to the Ordinary
Diocese of Georgia
Savannah, Georgia

The Way of Love

Questions

Have you wished God would punish rather than forgive some person or group?

When have you been sure of what you wanted God to do, only to have your wish fail to be granted?

How have you experienced being changed by prayer over time?

Prayer

Most gracious God whose ways are not our ways and whose thoughts are not our thoughts, pour into our hearts an abundance of your love, that we may delight in your will and walk in your ways; through Jesus Christ our Savior. *Amen.*

Worship

Luke 24:28-35

[28]As they came near the village to which they were going, he walked ahead as if he were going on. [29]But they urged him strongly, saying, "Stay with us, because it is almost evening and the day is now nearly over." So he went in to stay with them. [30]When he was at the table with them, he took bread, blessed and broke it, and gave it to them. [31]Then their eyes were opened, and they recognized him; and he vanished from their sight. [32]They said to each other, "Were not our hearts burning within us while he was talking to us on the road, while he was opening the scriptures to us?" [33]That same hour they got up and returned to Jerusalem; and they found the eleven and their companions gathered together. [34]They were saying, "The Lord has risen indeed, and he has appeared to Simon!" [35]Then they told what had happened on the road, and how he had been made known to them in the breaking of the bread.

Reflection

Luke 24 is a story that follows the pattern of eucharist. A guest becomes the host who takes, blesses, breaks, and gives bread with two along the way whose eyes are opened to the presence of the one they call Lord. Two disciples are comforted in an intimate meal.

So often we focus on this comfort. Today, let us instead remain with the reality of grief for these travelers. The two disciples have witnessed the execution of the one whom they had believed would deliver Israel. Grief-stricken and confused, they walk alongside Jesus yet cannot see him. Life and death, presence and absence, permeate the narrative. The community of believers has been dealt a severe blow and struggles to find meaning in the aftermath of Jesus' death.

Such trauma is the reality of so many today, people who live on the edge of society: men, women, and children in prisons and in cages along our borders; families sleeping in tents under highways; mothers and fathers arrested with worry for their black children; the elderly lonely and isolated in care facilities. This story, this Road to Emmaus story, offers the possibility of new life amid trauma. Jesus meets the two disciples in the midst of their trauma, and Jesus meets us in ours. If we listen, Jesus will recount the story of God's love. If we open the door and invite him in, Jesus will nourish our lives. But we must first offer our lives, our grief, and even our confusion—and that of those around us. We must invite others to taste and see. Who is the Jesus among us? Jesus comes to us as the marginalized, oppressed, and disenfranchised. Invite the stranger to be in your midst as host; be fed and have your eyes opened. Such is an act of worship.

The Rev. Jenifer Gamber
Assistant Rector and Chaplain to the Day School
St. Patrick's Episcopal Church
Washington, D.C.

Questions

Recall a time you came to the table of Holy Eucharist with the fullness of your life. How were you nourished?

When have you been surprised by God in the hospitality of a stranger?

Prayer

O God, whose blessed Son made himself known to his disciples in the breaking of bread: Open the eyes of our faith, that we may behold him in all his redeeming work; who lives and reigns with you, in the unity of the Holy Spirit, one God, now and for ever. *Amen.*

—*The Book of Common Prayer,* p. 223

Isaiah 2:1-5

¹The word that Isaiah son of Amoz saw concerning Judah and Jerusalem. ²In days to come the mountain of the LORD's house shall be established as the highest of the mountains, and shall be raised above the hills; all the nations shall stream to it. ³Many peoples shall come and say, "Come, let us go up to the mountain of the LORD, to the house of the God of Jacob; that he may teach us his ways and that we may walk in his paths."

For out of Zion shall go forth instruction, and the word of the LORD from Jerusalem. ⁴He shall judge between the nations, and shall arbitrate for many peoples; they shall beat their swords into plowshares, and their spears into pruning hooks; nation shall not lift up sword against nation, neither shall they learn war any more.

⁵O house of Jacob, come, let us walk in the light of the LORD!

Reflection

For the prophet Isaiah, faith can never be a purely private matter. Isaiah believes worship changes us and has the power and indeed the intention to change the world. Fortunately, Isaiah's lofty expectation is matched by a clear understanding of how such change is fostered. He speaks first of the Lord's house being raised above the hills. One really does go up to Jerusalem from the surrounding plains, and the temple actually towers above the ancient city. This geography is a word to us: God is meant to be above all else and worship our priority.

More compelling still is Isaiah's insistence that for the world to be redeemed, all the nations must be drawn into this worship. The temple is magnificent in its splendor and so a draw for visitors to the ancient city. But that's curiosity, not worship. Isaiah says the nations will come to the temple because people want to learn about the Lord and "walk in his paths."

To come to worship in our day is itself an act of faith. Those who take that step, whether they can verbalize it or not, hope to encounter the living God. This hope ignites the desire to live in new ways, but the flame of desire must be tended. This is why worship demands a community. Those new to faith need the prayers of those who have walked with Jesus for years. Those who find their passion for the gospel subsiding need to pray alongside those who are on fire with the love of God. When we feel alone in the world, worship reminds us of the communion of saints that surround us, encouraging us to fulfill our call to make the love of Christ tangible and visible—and to change the world.

None of this is easy. Isaiah knows that. Beating swords into plowshares requires the ability to see a whole new reality, God's reality. But it is holy work—and worship, where we see one another made new is where the work begins. For us and for the sake of the world.

The Rev. Jenifer Gamber
Assistant Rector and Chaplain to the Day School
St. Patrick's Episcopal Church
Washington, D.C.

Questions

Have you been changed through worship? In what ways? How has this change been nurtured? Or if it hasn't, how can you find new ways to revive it?

If someone asked you why you go to church, what would you tell them?

Do people know where your church is located? Can they find their way in? Will they be welcomed? What might you do to make your church community a beacon that draws people to Christ?

Prayer

Almighty God, in the abundance of your love, you have given yourself to us through your Son Jesus and welcomed us as disciples. Keep us faithful to that calling that all we meet might see and know your love has no limit. All this we ask, knowing that we are held fast in Christ's saving embrace. *Amen.*

Isaiah 29:13

[13]The LORD said: Because these people draw near with their mouths and honor me with their lips, while their hearts are far from me, and their worship of me is a human commandment learned by rote.

Reflection

In many churches, among people who lead liturgy there's a lot of shoptalk about doing worship "right"—whether that means rattling off the prayers perfectly, making sure the color of the flowers matches the shade of the chasubles, or teaching acolytes to reverence the altar with the precision of synchronized swimmers. At St. Gregory of Nyssa Episcopal Church, where I served for ten years, we talked about the importance of doing worship "well" instead of "right"—singing boldly, speaking clearly, praying aloud honestly.

While it still makes me twitch when I hear a preacher overshare cute stories about his kids, or see a communion server yank the chalice away abruptly from an unsteady person, or endure endless moments of awkward silence while an officiant tries to remember her place in the script, I've mostly been freed from the constant drone of liturgical fine-tuning in my head that preoccupied me when I saw myself as a worship leader. I still have plenty of opinions about the amazing array of stylistic choices different churches make, and I still cling to personal preferences—but now, I mostly care less that worship is done right or well and more that it is real.

Real worship doesn't start with any human rules or words or lip service: It starts with God's own desire to enter human hearts and change us. Real worship has the power to reveal real relationship with God; it tunes our hearts, sometimes to breaking and always to grace.

Sara Miles
Author and Social Justice Activist
San Francisco, California

Questions

What are the "human rules" you've been taught about worship?

When have you felt that you were honoring God only with your lips? When have you experienced worship that has brought your heart closer to God?

Prayer

O God, who created humankind to worship you: Inscribe your Word so deeply in our hearts that we may be freed from human rules, led by your Holy Spirit, and bound to you always, through the love of Jesus Christ our Lord. *Amen.*

Psalm 96:1-9

1   Sing to the LORD a new song; *
        sing to the LORD, all the whole earth.

2   Sing to the LORD and bless his Name; *
        proclaim the good news of his salvation from day to day.

3   Declare his glory among the nations *
        and his wonders among all peoples.

4   For great is the LORD and greatly to be praised; *
        he is more to be feared than all gods.

5   As for all the gods of the nations, they are but idols; *
        but it is the LORD who made the heavens.

6   Oh, the majesty and magnificence of his presence! *
        Oh, the power and the splendor of his sanctuary!

7   Ascribe to the LORD, you families of the peoples; *
        ascribe to the LORD honor and power.

8   Ascribe to the LORD the honor due his Name; *
        bring offerings and come into his courts.

9   Worship the LORD in the beauty of holiness; *
        let the whole earth tremble before him.

Reflection

Some years ago, I lived in a small college town on the coast of Lake Michigan. The area was prone to storms year round, and while lake-effect snow was terrifying, the thunderstorms and high winds were a better reminder of my mortality.

West Michigan storms are full sensory experiences: The sky turns a sickening shade of grey-green, and tornado sirens mix with sharp thunderclaps. Lightning forks across the sky in ever-shorter intervals, the temperature falls, and any humidity—suffocating when the storm began—disappears. Then, after shaking the earth, the storms end.

After one of these late afternoon storms, I drove toward the lake, weaving around fallen branches and broken tulips, breathing in the cool, wet air, smelling the hopeful scent of earthworms and dirt. As I headed west, the sun came out at such an angle that it bathed everything in a golden light. The grass was gold. The road was gold. A family of deer stepping out of the forest glowed gold. The sky and the ground were gold, and when I looked at my face in the mirror, I was gold, too. In that junk car, I believe I saw all the world joyfully crying out to their maker. And I laughed, knowing that I would never see something as glorious the rest of my life.

Worship the Lord in the splendor of his holiness, a light so radiant, an arm so powerful, a love so consuming. Walk on the warm earth; stand beneath the heavens and their innumerable stars and know that long before you walked here and long after you go to sleep, the song goes on, ever new.

Christopher Sikkema
Manager for Special Projects
The Episcopal Church
Rochester, Minnesota

Questions

Where have you experienced the splendor of God's holiness?

A quotation attributed to Saint Irenaeus of Lyons says, "The glory of God is [the human person] fully alive." Is this true in your experience? Do you think this is applicable across creation?

Prayer

Lord of storm clouds and thunderbolts, creator of shining light and enfolding dark, help us to glorify you in the moments of dread and beauty. Remind us that even as we tremble before your majesty, your property is always to have mercy. Draw us ever closer in worship to you and your creation. *Amen*.

1 Corinthians 11:23-26

23For I received from the Lord what I also handed on to you, that the Lord Jesus on the night when he was betrayed took a loaf of bread, 24and when he had given thanks, he broke it and said, "This is my body that is for you. Do this in remembrance of me." 25In the same way he took the cup also, after supper, saying, "This cup is the new covenant in my blood. Do this, as often as you drink it, in remembrance of me." 26For as often as you eat this bread and drink the cup, you proclaim the Lord's death until he comes.

Reflection

Worship is important to Episcopalians, for good reason. It's not uncommon to hear that worship inspires us and imbues life with meaning, and it clearly binds us in community as well. Yet scripture says surprisingly little about worship, at least in the sense we tend to use the term. "Worship" language in the Bible tends to be used not about ritual, music, or meetings but rather in reference to obedience and service. Worship in the Bible has as much to do with ethics as liturgy.

Yet there are clear New Testament models for joining in prayer and for gathering as a community, and clear commands by Jesus have led to the characteristic Christian practice of Holy Eucharist. The words prayed over bread and wine from Jesus, through Saint Paul, are among the most often heard in our characteristic worship.

Worship itself isn't our call; truth be told, everyone worships something, whether ritually or communally or otherwise. What makes our worship distinctive isn't the ritual itself but the One whom we serve.

"Do this in remembrance of me" is a command to gather and to share in a meal whose character defines our worship in every sense—following Paul's account of Jesus' supper, we take, bless, and share. Doing all this, we are remembering him, his life, death, and resurrection, as we are called to do.

The middle of these three actions, the "giving thanks," gives our liturgy its name, *eucharistia*. This underrated idea says something fundamental, not just about worship in the narrow sense but in the deepest and widest sense: We live in thanksgiving, in gratitude, to

The Way of Love

the One who is the source of all our being as well as the source of our salvation. Remembering Jesus specifically by the action of giving thanks at the eucharist, we express and reinforce the character of our relationship with God in every meal, and every moment.

The Very Rev. Dr. Andrew McGowan
Dean and President
Berkeley Divinity School at Yale
New Haven, Connecticut

Questions

What would it mean to live "eucharistically"—with thanks, in all things?

How and where do we see our lives reflected in the liturgy? How and where do we see see liturgy reflected in our lives?

Prayer

God, you have called us to be the body of your Son Jesus Christ: Take, bless, break, and distribute us, so we may be your love in the world and serve you as you would have us do. *Amen*.

Acts 2:42-47

42 They devoted themselves to the apostles' teaching and fellowship, to the breaking of bread and the prayers.

43 Awe came upon everyone, because many wonders and signs were being done by the apostles. 44 All who believed were together and had all things in common; 45 they would sell their possessions and goods and distribute the proceeds to all, as any had need. 46 Day by day, as they spent much time together in the temple, they broke bread at home and ate their food with glad and generous hearts, 47 praising God and having the goodwill of all the people. And day by day the Lord added to their number those who were being saved.

Reflection

A common love creates a common ground that has room enough for all of us to stand. Let that love be the love of Jesus.
—Presiding Bishop Michael B. Curry

The passage from Acts is one of my favorites. Maybe this is because it names so many of my favorite things: sharing meals, being with friends, helping others, praying together. But it is the "together" part that speaks most directly to my heart.

The Voice translation of the Bible includes this phrase: "There was an intense sense of togetherness among all who believed." I love the images this evokes—I think of Ron, Harry, and Hermione in the *Harry Potter* series as they fought the dark forces together, the 2012 United States Women's Soccer team when they took the gold medal, and all of those closing summer camp eucharists when the tears flow for everyone, campers and counselors alike. Something about gathering around a common love changes us—it changes our perception of ourselves, of those on the journey with us, and perhaps of those outside the journey.

We encounter the love of Jesus in many ways. Some of us feel God most personally in solitary moments—in nature, in prayer, in artistic endeavors, or on retreat; still, worshiping in "one accord" is an essential part of living a baptized life. From the beginning of our origin story we hear these words, "It is not good that the man should be alone; I will make him a helper as his partner" (Genesis 2:18). As a species—and as believers—we have been created to be in community.

Corporate worship provides the opportunity for all of us to stand on common ground together. Each week we leave our silos—our individual practices of worship, our fears of not being accepted or accepting, our different affiliations—and choose to live into the love of Jesus together. We come to the table, which has room enough for everyone, and where, through the power of the Holy Spirit, we are made one body sent forth to live the Way of Love.

Jerusalem Greer
Staff Officer for Evangelism ·
The Episcopal Church
Greenbrier, Arkansas

Questions

When have you been part of a team or group that shared an intense common love? How did that love create common ground despite differences? When have you felt that same intensity around worship or love of God?

How do you best connect with the love of Jesus? Is it in nature? Through learning? Through the arts? Through conversation with others? How can you share this way of connecting with others? Is there a way to bring others along with you in the experience so that you find common ground?

Prayer

Almighty Father, whose blessed Son before his passion prayed for his disciples that they might be one, as you and he are one: Grant that your Church, being bound together in love and obedience to you, may be united in one body by the one Spirit, that the world may believe in him whom you have sent, your Son Jesus Christ our Lord; who lives and reigns with you, in the unity of the Holy Spirit, one God, now and for ever. *Amen.*

—*The Book of Common Prayer,* p. 255

The Way of Love

John 4:7-26

[7]A Samaritan woman came to draw water, and Jesus said to her, "Give me a drink." [8](His disciples had gone to the city to buy food.) [9]The Samaritan woman said to him, "How is it that you, a Jew, ask a drink of me, a woman of Samaria?" (Jews do not share things in common with Samaritans.)

[10]Jesus answered her, "If you knew the gift of God, and who it is that is saying to you, 'Give me a drink,' you would have asked him, and he would have given you living water." [11]The woman said to him, "Sir, you have no bucket, and the well is deep. Where do you get that living water? [12]Are you greater than our ancestor Jacob, who gave us the well, and with his sons and his flocks drank from it?" [13]Jesus said to her, "Everyone who drinks of this water will be thirsty again, [14]but those who drink of the water that I will give them will never be thirsty. The water that I will give will become in them a spring of water gushing up to eternal life." [15]The woman said to him, "Sir, give me this water, so that I may never be thirsty or have to keep coming here to draw water."

[16]Jesus said to her, "Go, call your husband, and come back." [17]The woman answered him, "I have no husband." Jesus said to her, "You are right in saying, 'I have no husband'; [18]for you have had five husbands, and the one you have now is not your husband. What you have said is true!" [19]The woman said to him, "Sir, I see that you are a prophet. [20]Our ancestors worshiped on this mountain, but you say that the place where people must worship is in Jerusalem." [21]Jesus said to her, "Woman, believe me, the hour is coming when

you will worship the Father neither on this mountain nor in Jerusalem. ²²You worship what you do not know; we worship what we know, for salvation is from the Jews. ²³But the hour is coming, and is now here, when the true worshipers will worship the Father in spirit and truth, for the Father seeks such as these to worship him. ²⁴God is spirit, and those who worship him must worship in spirit and truth." ²⁵The woman said to him, "I know that Messiah is coming" (who is called Christ). "When he comes, he will proclaim all things to us." ²⁶Jesus said to her, "I am he, the one who is speaking to you."

Reflection

When trying to form disciples for Jesus Christ, I am always hoping people will have some sort of encounter with the Risen Lord. In these verses, we see one of the stranger and amazing encounters anyone has with Jesus. As my grandmother would say, "He read her mail!"

At the 2019 Forma conference, the Rev. Marcus Halley challenged our attendees to believe that they would truly encounter God in worship. It's a tall order, really. Think about it. When was the last time you entered worship with the expectation that you would encounter God? Have you ever had that expectation?

We are told that Jesus is present with us in the breaking of the bread, when two or three are gathered, and in many other ways through worship and praise. Why don't we believe it? What is holding us back? God doesn't make promises and then break them.

This back and forth between Jesus and the Samaritan woman has many implications and offers several compelling lessons for preaching and teaching. I'd like to focus on just a small component of the story. One of the delightful moments in this passage occurs when the woman asks Jesus to give her this water so that she doesn't have to keep coming back to fill her jars! It reads a bit like a joke. She wants this pest of a man to do something for her to make her life easier and better.

How many of us approach Jesus the same way? Have you ever prayed to God to make your life a little easier and a little better? Has God ever answered you like Jesus answered this woman? I bet the answer is yes. I bet that God has "read your mail" back to you more than once!

This brings us to a key verse: "But the hour is coming, and is now here, when the true worshipers will worship the Father in spirit and truth, for the Father seeks such as these to worship him." God is not a stationary God. We don't only worship God at the mountain or in Jerusalem. We worship God in every place and with our every word. We worship God in church, at work, at school, and at home. There is no easy cure to make our lives easier or better, just the promise that God is present in our everyday lives—and always when we worship.

Bill Campbell
Executive Director
Forma
Alexandria, Virginia

The Way of Love

Questions

Do you expect to encounter God when you worship?

What would you need to change in order to have this expectation?

Prayer

Jesus, you came to us in the form of a man and lived as God among us. Send your presence to surround us and all who gather so that we might know your embrace. Give us confidence in your promise that you are here. Strengthen our faith so that we may learn to live in worship in your eternal presence. *Amen.*

Bless

Matthew 10:1-15

[1]Then Jesus summoned his twelve disciples and gave them authority over unclean spirits, to cast them out, and to cure every disease and every sickness. [2]These are the names of the twelve apostles: first, Simon, also known as Peter, and his brother Andrew; James son of Zebedee, and his brother John; [3]Philip and Bartholomew; Thomas and Matthew the tax collector; James son of Alphaeus, and Thaddaeus; [4]Simon the Cananaean, and Judas Iscariot, the one who betrayed him.

[5]These twelve Jesus sent out with the following instructions: "Go nowhere among the Gentiles, and enter no town of the Samaritans, [6]but go rather to the lost sheep of the house of Israel. [7]As you go, proclaim the good news, 'The kingdom of heaven has come near.' [8]Cure the sick, raise the dead, cleanse the lepers, cast out demons. You received without payment; give without payment. [9]Take no gold, or silver, or copper in your belts, [10]no bag for your journey, or two tunics, or sandals, or a staff; for laborers deserve their food. [11]Whatever town or village you enter, find out who in it is worthy, and stay there until you leave. [12]As you enter the house, greet it. [13]If the house is worthy, let your peace come upon it; but if it is not worthy, let your peace return to you. [14]If anyone will not welcome you or listen to your words, shake off the dust from your feet as you leave that house or town. [15]Truly I tell you, it will be more tolerable for the land of Sodom and Gomorrah on the day of judgment than for that town."

Reflection

When the disciples head out on their mission they are told to take no bag for the journey, no extra shirt or sandals or a staff. Packing that light only makes sense if you are traveling in community and you believe you will make friends along the way. These disciples are going to need someone to offer them an extra shirt, a cup of water, and a place to rest their weary heads. The truth that they will be relying on one another and the strangers they encounter is a mark that this is going to be a healing journey. If they pack all they need, they won't need one another or new friends.

There is a freedom and joy to packing light, expecting that the community you encounter will be sufficient. You can offer some tiny bit of what God has offered to you and receive with deep gratitude the offerings of a fellow pilgrim. In such a scenario, we all are givers and receivers, and love is found in the exchange. The disciples offer good news to the poor that sets captives free and heals suffering. In exchange, they make friends, find community, and are sustained.

I have seen this story of healing on a journey lived out a thousand times. Through my work at Thistle Farms, a global community of survivors of trafficking and addiction, I have seen women walk in from the streets with nothing to their names, not even a change of clothes, and encounter the promise that while they begin to heal, a community will take care of their needs. They don't have a purse or two pairs of sandals yet these beloved disciples accept the offer, and within months you can see the brave women survivors offering shirts, bedspreads, and extra shoes to other women seeking healing.

My most vivid memory of experiencing the healing power of traveling light came when I arrived in Ecuador on a site visit to a school and social enterprise we started in the Los Rios area. By accident I had left out my clothes from my bag when I put costumes in for a school play we were putting on. For that whole week, I had never dressed so nice or felt so loved. Everyone offered things from their bags, and in community, I was fine with no clothes in the middle of the Ecuador!

In order to pack lighter and make room for community, we have to believe that our needs can be swallowed up in God's abundance. I once heard that there is enough food in the world to feed all the hungry children. It is not a lack of resources—simply a lack of will. When I think about what I have stuffed into my bags because of fear and thinking in scarcity, it causes me great grief. Maybe we can all pack, store, and buy this year with a more trusting heart.

The Rev. Becca Stevens
Founder and President
Thistle Farms
Nashville, Tennessee

The Way of Love

Questions

Can you try for one trip or one week to pack less into your bags or refrigerator as a sign of a more healing journey, one open to community?

Is there a person who has fed and clothed you on your journey that you could offer thanks for today?

Prayer

Gracious and loving God with whom our journey begins and ends, help us to remember that you have given us all that we have. Everything we have is yours, and it is our gift to share it with one another in community. Open our eyes and hands to see the world around us and to accept when we are hungry and to feed others when we are sated. *Amen.*

Deuteronomy 8:10-17

[10]You shall eat your fill and bless the LORD your God for the good land that he has given you.

[11]Take care that you do not forget the LORD your God, by failing to keep his commandments, his ordinances, and his statutes, which I am commanding you today. [12]When you have eaten your fill and have built fine houses and live in them, [13]and when your herds and flocks have multiplied, and your silver and gold is multiplied, and all that you have is multiplied, [14]then do not exalt yourself, forgetting the LORD your God, who brought you out of the land of Egypt, out of the house of slavery, [15]who led you through the great and terrible wilderness, an arid wasteland with poisonous snakes and scorpions. He made water flow for you from flint rock, [16]and fed you in the wilderness with manna that your ancestors did not know, to humble you and to test you, and in the end to do you good. [17]Do not say to yourself, "My power and the might of my own hand have gotten me this wealth."

Reflection

Moses is pretty clear. He usually is. These verses from his farewell discourse to the people he has led for forty years, people about to enter the promised land without him, is to the point: There is an amazing future ahead of you, but never forget who gave you this land or what it took to get you here. Good advice—and most of us have heard or given a version of it: Don't forget where you came from and who helped you along the way.

With all that talk of flocks and land and food, it's clear Moses is talking to people who will set up agricultural communities. But he knows—though they can't yet—that if they flourish, flocks and herds may be supplanted, at least for some, by gold and silver and real estate. I almost expected him to include stocks and bonds. He speaks to the people as they look over the Jordan river; he speaks to us, whatever our vantage point.

Remembering where I've come from and all the help, correction, and encouragement I've received from God and from people along the way helps keep me thankful, grounded, and able to offer support to others. But while Moses knows that memory and gratitude are important aids to remembering God and helping others, he also knows they are insufficient on their own. We need regular, daily disciplines. That's what keeps us blessing God and others for a lifetime.

Commandments, ordinances, and statutes. Hardly poetic, but they pave the way to creating the communion of saints. Read the Bible, say our prayers, support those in need, and let ourselves be supported when we are in need. We start there, remembering Jesus' helpful summary: He said to him, "'You shall love the Lord your God with all your heart, and with all your soul, and with all your mind.' This is the greatest and first commandment. And a second is like it: 'You shall love your neighbor as yourself'" (Matthew 22:37-39). Do these things, and we will know just how blessed we are. Do these things and our neighbors shall know themselves blessed as well.

The Rev. Brenda Husson
Rector, St. James' Church
New York City, New York

Questions _____

Which of the ten commandments do you have the most trouble keeping? Why do you think that is? What practice might you undertake to help build that commandment into your life?

Which people have been blessings to you? In what ways did they model Jesus' summary of the law for you? If they are still alive, find a way to tell them what a gift they gave you. If they are not, offer a prayer in thanksgiving for their part in your life.

Prayer _____

God of all our days, I thank you for Jesus' promise to be with me in my daily walk, whether I run with joy or can barely move for sorrow. Grant me the grace and the courage to become a faithful companion to others in their journey and show me the ways I can best serve you in serving others. I offer this prayer trusting in your never-failing love. *Amen.*

Ephesians 3:14-21

[14]For this reason I bow my knees before the Father, [15]from whom every family in heaven and on earth takes its name. [16]I pray that, according to the riches of his glory, he may grant that you may be strengthened in your inner being with power through his Spirit, [17]and that Christ may dwell in your hearts through faith, as you are being rooted and grounded in love. [18]I pray that you may have the power to comprehend, with all the saints, what is the breadth and length and height and depth, [19]and to know the love of Christ that surpasses knowledge, so that you may be filled with all the fullness of God.

[20]Now to him who by the power at work within us is able to accomplish abundantly far more than all we can ask or imagine, [21]to him be glory in the church and in Christ Jesus to all generations, forever and ever. Amen.

Reflection

One of the most profound practices we share as Christians is to bless one another, and we do this by becoming participants in the flow of Christ's love in the world. The word "bless" comes from the Old English *bletsian*, "to consecrate by a religious rite, make holy, give thanks," and in exploring this practice, we might consider Paul's prayer to the church at Ephesus that "Christ may dwell in your hearts through faith, as you are being rooted and grounded in love."

What does it mean to be "rooted and grounded in love?" For me it means that when the storms of life come and the winds of despair threaten to take away my hopes and dreams, I am safely rooted in the soil of God's gracious love and forgiveness. And although I may bend with the weight of pain and suffering, in the end I will not break because I am grounded in the love of Christ.

From the depths of our personal brokenness and depression God will give us a life of joy, purpose, and meaning, and it is our call as Christians to reach out and help (bless) those around us who might also be in the depths of loneliness and despair. Author Anne Lamott expands this thought, saying, "If you are no longer in bondage to a person or a way of life, tell your story. Risk freeing someone else."

It's risky business to confront our fears and share our story, but by doing so we are a blessing to those who might need our words of encouragement. Acknowledging with compassion the pain and suffering of others is one way that we bless those around us, and God will give us the strength and courage we need. We need only ask!

Mary Foster Parmer
Creator and Director, Invite Welcome Connect
Beecken Center of the School of Theology, University of the South
Sewanee, Tennessee

Questions

Author Anne Lamott speaks of freeing someone else by sharing our story. In what ways is this true for you?

When have you been blessed by another's loving kindness and compassionate act? Do you consciously make an intentional effort to bless others with your story?

Prayer

Strengthen us, O God, with the power of your Spirit. Give us courage to face our demons and find redemption and healing in the sacred soil of your love and forgiveness. Grant us the fortitude to risk freeing others by sharing our stories of grace and peace. *Amen.*

Jeremiah 7:1-7

¹The word that came to Jeremiah from the LORD: ²Stand in the gate of the LORD's house, and proclaim there this word, and say, Hear the word of the LORD, all you people of Judah, you that enter these gates to worship the LORD. ³Thus says the LORD of hosts, the God of Israel: Amend your ways and your doings, and let me dwell with you in this place. ⁴Do not trust in these deceptive words: "This is the temple of the LORD, the temple of the LORD, the temple of the LORD."

⁵For if you truly amend your ways and your doings, if you truly act justly one with another, ⁶if you do not oppress the alien, the orphan, and the widow, or shed innocent blood in this place, and if you do not go after other gods to your own hurt, ⁷then I will dwell with you in this place, in the land that I gave of old to your ancestors forever and ever.

Reflection

In the time of ancient Israel, religion was just as complicated and diverse as we find it today. Though the kingdom of Judah was Jewish, what that meant and how that should be best expressed was a topic of intense debate.

One popular take on religion of the day held that really, it was a *fait accompli*. Because God had blessed Israel with the temple under King Solomon, the temple alone was such a sign of divine favor that as long as it stood and as long as worship was performed properly there, nothing else mattered. God surely dwelt with Israel in his temple; so long as that was the case, the kingdom would never falter.

Jeremiah, clearly, does not hold this view. God sends him word that he is to literally stand at the gates of the temple and announce to all who pass by that God demands more. God demands justice, mercy, and love of neighbor. God asks us for an outward-looking faith, one that seeks to share with others the bounty of blessings we have received, and not to simply bask in the presence of God. Absent these things, we do not have a right relationship with God, no matter how exalted our piety or how exquisite our liturgy.

Jeremiah reminds us that to be in right relationship with God requires being in right relationship with others and vice versa. We cannot trade one for the other. Each day, our faith compels us to check on the welfare of both relationships and hold both sacred—and when we fall short in either, to repent and make amends.

The Rev. Megan L. Castellan
Rector
St. John's Episcopal Church
Ithaca, New York

The Way of Love

Questions

Do you find it easier to focus on worshiping God or serving others? Why? How have you experienced God through other people?

How have you experienced worship as an act of service and blessing? How might the two be connected?

Prayer

God of beauty and of justice, you draw our attention both inward and outward: Remind us that our focus on you must always direct our love to your creation and that our attention to your creation must always bring us back to you, the source of all, through Christ our Lord. *Amen.*

Romans 12:9-21

⁹Let love be genuine; hate what is evil, hold fast to what is good; ¹⁰love one another with mutual affection; outdo one another in showing honor. ¹¹Do not lag in zeal, be ardent in spirit, serve the Lord. ¹²Rejoice in hope, be patient in suffering, persevere in prayer. ¹³Contribute to the needs of the saints; extend hospitality to strangers.

¹⁴Bless those who persecute you; bless and do not curse them. ¹⁵Rejoice with those who rejoice, weep with those who weep. ¹⁶Live in harmony with one another; do not be haughty, but associate with the lowly; do not claim to be wiser than you are. ¹⁷Do not repay anyone evil for evil, but take thought for what is noble in the sight of all. ¹⁸If it is possible, so far as it depends on you, live peaceably with all. ¹⁹Beloved, never avenge yourselves, but leave room for the wrath of God; for it is written, "Vengeance is mine, I will repay, says the Lord." ²⁰No, "if your enemies are hungry, feed them; if they are thirsty, give them something to drink; for by doing this you will heap burning coals on their heads." ²¹Do not be overcome by evil, but overcome evil with good.

Reflection

In this portion of his letter to the church in Rome, Paul packs twenty-three imperatives of the Christian life in a mere thirteen verses. The lists are exhausting and seemingly impossible. But are they? Each directive is an expression of one overarching imperative: Love one another. "Let love be genuine," says Paul and continues by naming acts of genuine love—mutual affection, honor, patience in suffering, perseverance in prayer, humility. Such acts are not outside our reach. In fact the reach itself is not ours but God's. "Love one another as I have loved you," Jesus says in John 13:34.

These imperatives describe a life of blessing, a life transformed by God's love. Receiving God's love and loving in return as blessing is transformational and countercultural. In the name of self-preservation, society prefers isolation rather than blessing. We so easily turn inward rather than take the risk of extending hospitality to others.

In southeast Washington, D.C., a subsidized housing complex that is home for four hundred families is surrounded by an eight-foot prison-grade fence, in the name of safety for its residents. Families seeking asylum in America's southern border are separated and encaged, in the name of security. Christians are called to extend hospitality and cross boundaries by tearing down walls, not building them.

The words "hospitality," "host," "hostile," and "hostage" all derive from the Latin root *hostis*, meaning stranger or enemy. As Christians we are called to bless others in acts of hospitality, risking safety and security to expand the circle to include strangers and even our enemies, opening the possibility that stranger and enemy alike may become friend. In the basement of that D.C. housing complex, inside the eight-foot fence, is a suite of brightly colored rooms filled with caring professionals attending to the needs of the children and the families who call that place home. They are doing the hard work of giving and receiving blessings and expanding the circle from the inside out. Saint Paul calls the church to such genuine love.

The Rev. Jenifer Gamber
Assistant Rector and Chaplain to the Day School
St. Patrick's Episcopal Church
Washington, D.C.

Questions _____

When have you or your church expanded the circle from the inside out? What boundaries expanded? How did it transform your life or the life of others?

Look at the list of imperatives in the passage. Which expression of God's love are you challenged to enact in the world?

Prayer _____

God of compassion, we give thanks for Jesus, your Son, who sent his disciples to give, forgive, teach, and heal in his name. Help us to be genuine in our love, risking safety and security to bless those we might not ordinarily meet in our lives and to extend your love with words of hope and selfless acts. All this we ask in the name of your Son, Jesus Christ. *Amen.*

Isaiah 56:1-8

¹Thus says the LORD: Maintain justice, and do what is right, for soon my salvation will come, and my deliverance be revealed. ²Happy is the mortal who does this, the one who holds it fast, who keeps the sabbath, not profaning it, and refrains from doing any evil.

³Do not let the foreigner joined to the LORD say, "The LORD will surely separate me from his people"; and do not let the eunuch say, "I am just a dry tree." ⁴For thus says the LORD: To the eunuchs who keep my sabbaths, who choose the things that please me and hold fast my covenant, ⁵I will give, in my house and within my walls, a monument and a name better than sons and daughters; I will give them an everlasting name that shall not be cut off.

⁶And the foreigners who join themselves to the LORD, to minister to him, to love the name of the LORD, and to be his servants, all who keep the sabbath, and do not profane it, and hold fast my covenant— ⁷these I will bring to my holy mountain, and make them joyful in my house of prayer; their burnt offerings and their sacrifices will be accepted on my altar; for my house shall be called a house of prayer for all peoples. ⁸Thus says the Lord GOD, who gathers the outcasts of Israel, I will gather others to them besides those already gathered.

Reflection

With the advent of social media, one of the more ubiquitous hashtags is #blessed. But trying to discern a specific theology of blessedness from its proliferation might be difficult. Mostly, the hashtag sentiment conveys gratitude for basic luxuries of consumerism. Enjoying that latte? #blessed. Going to yoga? #blessed. Viewing a sunset? #blessed.

This basic understanding of blessedness, encouraged by American consumer culture, reduces the blessing of God to wishes granted and minimizes our life-giving relationship with the Divine into a transaction with a grumpy genie. But scripture reminds us that the blessedness of God is not about what we can receive from God. God doesn't bless us with various tokens of prosperity and pleasing photo opportunities. God blesses us so that we can go out and serve others.

Indeed, when Isaiah talks about blessedness, the entire point is to bless others. Israel is named as the chosen people in order to bless the world, to welcome it to the mountain of God—not to keep it for themselves. The blessings of God are always meant to transform us so that we can transform the world. They are never for self alone. God is less interested in making sure you have a great espresso and more interested that you are so grateful for that espresso that you extend kindness and love to the person who made it for you. In Isaiah's vision of the mountain of God, this blessedness becomes a way to welcome all creation to the presence of God. It is not a justification for division or for separation of the haves from the have-nots. When God blesses us, our task is to turn and welcome those around us to share in our blessedness. Our task is to bless the world.

The Rev. Megan L. Castellan
Rector
St. John's Episcopal Church
Ithaca, New York

Questions

What blessings are you particularly cognizant of today? How have you used these gifts to enable the ministry of others?

How have others used what they have to welcome and bless you?

Prayer

Almighty God, you have showered us with abundant blessings, such that we scarcely know how to number them: Teach us true gratitude, that we might become icons of your abundance in the world, and draw all people into your loving embrace, through Christ our Lord. *Amen.*

Jeremiah 29:11-14

[11]For surely I know the plans I have for you, says the LORD, plans for your welfare and not for harm, to give you a future with hope. [12]Then when you call upon me and come and pray to me, I will hear you. [13]When you search for me, you will find me; if you seek me with all your heart, [14]I will let you find me, says the LORD, and I will restore your fortunes and gather you from all the nations and all the places where I have driven you, says the LORD, and I will bring you back to the place from which I sent you into exile.

Reflection

There is a tradition in many *familias latinas* of asking for *la bendición* (a blessing). This request is made by a younger person to an older one or to someone who is admired, like a pastor. I love this tradition. "*Bendición*" we ask or is asked of us. "Please bless me." The person who blesses says, *Que Dios te bendiga* (May God bless you) and may say a prayer. Sometimes, the recipients will bow their heads and the giver will touch their head or make the sign of the cross on their head as they invoke a blessing. I have also seen people put their hands together as in prayer as the giver of the blessing blesses them.

The blessing given in this passage is one I love to receive and share with others who need it. A blessing is a balm, a healing touch, a loving embrace for anyone in need. God is blessing us with plans for a good and hopeful future, the certainty that God hears us when we call, the confidence that we will find God when we seek with all our heart, and the assurance that God will restore and reclaim us. This is great news that can impact people's lives today!

It is sometimes difficult to believe the blessings of goodness, hope, listening, presence, and restoration. Those of us who believe—who have faith—are to take the good news that Jesus wants to bless everyone to the world. Today's world is hurting. Today's world is hungry and desperate for freedom and respite. Today's world is broken. Today's world needs to be reminded that there is someone who wants to and can bless us.

Today's world is saying, "*Bendición*," as it bows its head, hoping someone will come to touch it and say, "*Que Dios te bendiga*."

Dr. Sandra T. Montes
Spanish Ministry Consultant and Musician
Sugar Land, Texas

Questions

How can you give someone *la bendición* today?

What *bendición* do you need?

Prayer

Dios, please give us your *bendición* of a hopeful future. Restore us and reclaim us daily as we go around the world giving the good news of your *bendición*. *En tu nombre. Amén.*

Go

John 20:19-29

¹⁹When it was evening on that day, the first day of the week, and the doors of the house where the disciples had met were locked for fear of the Jews, Jesus came and stood among them and said, "Peace be with you." ²⁰After he said this, he showed them his hands and his side. Then the disciples rejoiced when they saw the Lord. ²¹Jesus said to them again, "Peace be with you. As the Father has sent me, so I send you." ²²When he had said this, he breathed on them and said to them, "Receive the Holy Spirit. ²³If you forgive the sins of any, they are forgiven them; if you retain the sins of any, they are retained."

²⁴But Thomas (who was called the Twin), one of the twelve, was not with them when Jesus came. ²⁵So the other disciples told him, "We have seen the Lord." But he said to them, "Unless I see the mark of the nails in his hands, and put my finger in the mark of the nails and my hand in his side, I will not believe."

²⁶A week later his disciples were again in the house, and Thomas was with them. Although the doors were shut, Jesus came and stood among them and said, "Peace be with you." ²⁷Then he said to Thomas, "Put your finger here and see my hands. Reach out your hand and put it in my side. Do not doubt but believe." ²⁸Thomas answered him, "My Lord and my God!" ²⁹Jesus said to him, "Have you believed because you have seen me? Blessed are those who have not seen and yet have come to believe."

Reflection

That first spring, only a handful of farmers signed up for a blessing of the fields during Rogation Days. And even those few mostly did so out of respect for the priest, not out of a belief that the prayers and sprinkling of holy water would make any difference. But the priest dutifully and faithfully walked the bounds of the farms, praying and squirting holy water out of a bottle onto the freshly tilled soil.

Come fall, the farmers whose fields were blessed reported yields of 20 to 30 percent higher than their neighbors. Word soon spread about the priest and the holy water. The following spring, the sign-up list for Rogation Days ran three pages, with requests for prayers over fields and gardens and even flower beds. Like Thomas, they did not believe until they had seen a bountiful harvest of soybeans and corn—their equivalent of the mark of the nails.

Over the years, Thomas has gotten a bad rap, with people casting aspersions on his character and commitment because of his doubts. But I suspect many of us are like Thomas: We are willing to go, to act—we just need a little bit of proof. Why else would we bargain with God so often, making bold promises in exchange for some sort of sign? Jesus is gentle with Thomas, allowing him to touch the holes in his hands and the gash in his side. Despite the initial skepticism of the people, the priest didn't throw away the second-year list, full of folks primed for the blessings. However we get to the point of following Jesus, whether we have doubts or full-throttled faith, the important thing is that we are willing to go, to tell the story of the risen Christ to all who will hear, even and especially to those who will at first doubt.

Richelle Thompson
Deputy Director and Managing Editor
Forward Movement
Fort Thomas, Kentucky

Questions

Do you understand doubt primarily as a strength or a weakness? In what ways can asking questions enhance your faith and compel you to Go? In what ways can doubt impair your faith and keep you from taking action?

Have you ever bargained with God, asking for a sign so that you might be more certain in your faith? What do you think of Jesus' response to Thomas? How might you seek the blessing of believing without seeing?

Prayer

O God, by whom the meek are guided in judgment, and light rises up in darkness for the godly: Grant us, in all our doubts and uncertainties, the grace to ask what you would have us to do, that the Spirit of wisdom may save us from all false choices, and that in your light we may see light, and in your straight path may not stumble; through Jesus Christ our Lord. *Amen*.

—*The Book of Common Prayer*, p. 832

John 4:7-19

[7]A Samaritan woman came to draw water, and Jesus said to her, "Give me a drink." [8](His disciples had gone to the city to buy food.) [9]The Samaritan woman said to him, "How is it that you, a Jew, ask a drink of me, a woman of Samaria?" (Jews do not share things in common with Samaritans.) [10]Jesus answered her, "If you knew the gift of God, and who it is that is saying to you, 'Give me a drink,' you would have asked him, and he would have given you living water." [11]The woman said to him, "Sir, you have no bucket, and the well is deep. Where do you get that living water? [12]Are you greater than our ancestor Jacob, who gave us the well, and with his sons and his flocks drank from it?" [13]Jesus said to her, "Everyone who drinks of this water will be thirsty again, [14]but those who drink of the water that I will give them will never be thirsty. The water that I will give will become in them a spring of water gushing up to eternal life." [15]The woman said to him, "Sir, give me this water, so that I may never be thirsty or have to keep coming here to draw water."

[16]Jesus said to her, "Go, call your husband, and come back." [17]The woman answered him, "I have no husband." Jesus said to her, "You are right in saying, 'I have no husband'; [18]for you have had five husbands, and the one you have now is not your husband. What you have said is true!" [19]The woman said to him, "Sir, I see that you are a prophet."

Reflection

The Samaritan woman has a complicated marital history: five husbands! Perhaps that is why she comes to the well at noon instead of in the morning, when it is certain to be full of women and children drawing water for the day. You know what small towns are like; maybe the other women shun her, whisper to each other about her. Maybe she has had about enough of that.

She is not entirely truthful with this Jewish stranger about her current status. It is true that she has no husband, but she does not live alone. Still, she is honest enough to allow him to discern this painful part of her life, to give him a way into her isolation. And Jesus is honest enough, kind enough, respectful enough to go there with her: *I know exactly who you are, and it will not keep me from talking to you.* He speaks to her about theology, of all things. Most people don't speak to her at all.

She ends up forgetting all about her water jar and leaves it behind. It's heavy and awkward, and she is in a hurry. She must run to her village and tell everyone who she has seen! She has been transformed. She's not hiding from anybody now, not anymore. She thinks Jesus is a prophet. As she runs, she may not yet realize that she has just become one herself.

What kind of people does Christ send into the world to preach? Imperfect people, like the Samaritan woman at the well. People with things in their lives they wish weren't there. People like us.

The Rev. Barbara Cawthorne Crafton
Episcopal Priest and Author
Boulder, Colorado

Questions

Have you ever done something braver than you would have expected of yourself? Why were you surprised? Where did you think your courage came from at the time? Looking back now, do you see it the same way?

Has anyone ever surprised you by treating you with respect, perhaps someone who was supposed to be your enemy or someone you considered to rank far above you? Who was it? How did you respond?

When someone you know is revealed to have done something disgraceful, how do you behave toward that person? Do you reach out or stay away?

Prayer

Almighty God, to you all hearts are open, all desires known, and from you no secrets are hid: Cleanse the thoughts of our hearts by the inspiration of your Holy Spirit, that we may perfectly love you, and worthily magnify your holy Name; through Christ our Lord. *Amen.*

—*The Book of Common Prayer*, p. 355

Luke 10:1-11

[1]After this the Lord appointed seventy others and sent them on ahead of him in pairs to every town and place where he himself intended to go. [2]He said to them, "The harvest is plentiful, but the laborers are few; therefore ask the Lord of the harvest to send out laborers into his harvest. [3]Go on your way. See, I am sending you out like lambs into the midst of wolves. [4]Carry no purse, no bag, no sandals; and greet no one on the road. [5]Whatever house you enter, first say, 'Peace to this house!' [6]And if anyone is there who shares in peace, your peace will rest on that person; but if not, it will return to you.

[7]Remain in the same house, eating and drinking whatever they provide, for the laborer deserves to be paid. Do not move about from house to house. [8]Whenever you enter a town and its people welcome you, eat what is set before you; [9]cure the sick who are there, and say to them, 'The kingdom of God has come near to you.' [10]But whenever you enter a town and they do not welcome you, go out into its streets and say, [11]'Even the dust of your town that clings to our feet, we wipe off in protest against you. Yet know this: the kingdom of God has come near.'"

Reflection

What I find especially meaningful about this passage is that the "seventy others" Jesus sends out into the world are not discharged randomly to make their way as best they can, like pairs of honey bees leaving the hive in search of flowers. No, they are part of a larger plan. Jesus sends them ahead of him, to the places where he intends to go. In this sense, wherever they go, Jesus is right behind them, and they can trust that he is literally backing them up every step of the way.

I find this fact comforting. Whenever we step out in faith, into new situations, taking new risks to witness to Christ's love, we can rest assured that Christ follows behind us, making more of our efforts than if we were completely on our own. This means it isn't all about us and what *we* can accomplish; we are simply called to partner with Christ in Christ's work.

When I was a child, my father always dropped me off in front of our small church so I could save seats for the family while he parked the car. I would spread out my coat on a pew along with some bulletins and wait. I always felt so small and vulnerable as other adults began to fill the pews around me. But my job was simply to keep the space open, clinging to my father's promise that he and the other members of my family would be coming behind me to fill it in. In a similar way, whenever we step out as a witness for racial and social justice, speak up for peace, or care for someone who is lost, lonely, or in need, we may feel small and inadequate to the task. But we too have the promise that if we keep the space open, we won't be alone for long. Christ comes behind us to fill it in, to do the work he has come to do.

The Very Rev. Randolph Marshall Hollerith
Dean
Washington National Cathedral
Washington, D.C.

Questions

As you look at your daily life, how can you go ahead of Christ and create a space for him in the world?

In your life, what would it look like if you embraced the truth that you are one of the "seventy others"?

Outside of the people who are closest to you, how would anyone know that you are part of the Jesus Movement, that you are a follower of the Way of Love?

Prayer

Almighty and eternal God, so draw our hearts to thee, so guide our minds, so fill our imaginations, so control our wills, that we may be wholly thine, utterly dedicated unto thee; and then use us, we pray thee, as thou wilt, and always to thy glory and the welfare of thy people; through our Lord and Savior Jesus Christ. *Amen.*

—*The Book of Common Prayer,* p. 832

Luke 10:25-37

25Just then a lawyer stood up to test Jesus. "Teacher," he said, "what must I do to inherit eternal life?" 26He said to him, "What is written in the law? What do you read there?" 27He answered, "You shall love the Lord your God with all your heart, and with all your soul, and with all your strength, and with all your mind; and your neighbor as yourself." 28And he said to him, "You have given the right answer; do this, and you will live."

29But wanting to justify himself, he asked Jesus, "And who is my neighbor?" 30Jesus replied, "A man was going down from Jerusalem to Jericho, and fell into the hands of robbers, who stripped him, beat him, and went away, leaving him half dead. 31Now by chance a priest was going down that road; and when he saw him, he passed by on the other side. 32So likewise a Levite, when he came to the place and saw him, passed by on the other side. 33But a Samaritan while traveling came near him; and when he saw him, he was moved with pity. 34He went to him and bandaged his wounds, having poured oil and wine on them. Then he put him on his own animal, brought him to an inn, and took care of him. 35The next day he took out two denarii, gave them to the innkeeper, and said, 'Take care of him; and when I come back, I will repay you whatever more you spend.' 36Which of these three, do you think, was a neighbor to the man who fell into the hands of the robbers?" 37He said, "The one who showed him mercy." Jesus said to him, "Go and do likewise."

Reflection

I wonder what it would be like to live life to its fullest. Have you ever imagined yourself saying or doing things only to find that when the moment to take action comes, you shrink back because of the threat of embarrassment, afraid people won't understand you or fearful of being vulnerable? As courageous as I am in most of my life, in more instances than I'd like, I've learned to manage my vulnerability. Living life to its fullest is loving God, loving neighbor, and loving yourself with all your heart, and with all your soul, and with all your strength, and with all your mind! This kind of holy, holistic love makes our world bigger and God our neighbor. It makes us wholly human, seeing ourselves, others, and all creation through God's eyes. It's freeing and barrier-breaking. When we insist on this *Ubuntu*, "I am because you are," kind of love, society pushes back and reminds us to stay in our place, to view others with suspicion, and to believe in the lie of scarcity and self-preservation. Abundant love exposes us and leaves us naked. It is at once a defiant and vulnerable act. And it's costly, requiring us to invest our finances, time, and talents, as well as our physical, emotional, psychological, and spiritual energy.

When Jesus sees us lying on the road, beaten by sin, stripped naked from trying to live up to the world's standards that are never really achievable, half-dead from trying to do what we can never do on our own, he doesn't walk to the other side. Jesus comes alongside us and stays with us for a while. When he has to leave, he leaves provisions and promises to return. Jesus becomes entirely vulnerable for us so we might know what it means to have life, so we might feel what it is to be loved, and so we might go and do likewise. Go, love!

The Rev. Dr. Shannon MacVean-Brown
Interim Rector
St. Thomas Church
Franklin, Indiana

Questions _____

As much as it costs us to love, it costs us more when we don't. We are created to feel, notice, and love. How can you lovingly attend to the parts of you that you avoid: body, mind, spirit, and emotions?

The Good Samaritan invests in the wounded man. He invests time, finances, emotions, personal contact, and his body as he lifts and transports the hurt man. We all have our preferred ways of loving our neighbor. What are the ways that you love your neighbor? What are the ways you avoid investing in neighbor love?

Prayer _____

God of compassion, we thank you that in your abundant mercy, you have spared nothing to be our neighbor. In our quest for eternal life, you invite us to give ourselves—heart, body, mind, and spirit—to love. May the Holy Spirit lead us to an expanded understanding of neighbor and to a more authentic expression of love. We ask this through Jesus, your Son, who shows us the way to love you, our neighbor, and ourselves with our whole heart, and with all our soul, our strength, and our mind. *Amen.*

Isaiah 6:1-8

¹In the year that King Uzziah died, I saw the LORD sitting on a throne, high and lofty; and the hem of his robe filled the temple. ²Seraphs were in attendance above him; each had six wings: with two they covered their faces, and with two they covered their feet, and with two they flew. ³And one called to another and said: "Holy, holy, holy is the LORD of hosts; the whole earth is full of his glory." ⁴The pivots on the thresholds shook at the voices of those who called, and the house filled with smoke. ⁵And I said: "Woe is me! I am lost, for I am a man of unclean lips, and I live among a people of unclean lips; yet my eyes have seen the King, the LORD of hosts!"

⁶Then one of the seraphs flew to me, holding a live coal that had been taken from the altar with a pair of tongs. ⁷The seraph touched my mouth with it and said: "Now that this has touched your lips, your guilt has departed and your sin is blotted out." ⁸Then I heard the voice of the LORD saying, "Whom shall I send, and who will go for us?" And I said, "Here am I; send me!"

Reflection

Send me. I will go. I am a man of unclean lips, and I live among a people of unclean lips. But send me, and I will go, Isaiah says. In Isaiah's vision, seraphim praise God in his holiness, and those cries of glory leave him trembling and afraid. The prophet cites his sins and shortcomings, his unworthiness to be in God's presence. But the seraphim assure him of his worthiness, removing his guilt, and Isaiah moves from fear to boldly taking on the mantle of being a messenger of God.

This chapter ends with Isaiah's response, his willingness to go forth for God. He cannot understand how or why God will use him; he is not clean, not worthy. Isaiah's response truly is a leap of faith, a willingness to go where God is calling, without knowing where that call will lead.

We also do not know exactly where God's call will lead us, what is being asked of us, or how our life will change. But we do know this: God's call always leads us into sanctity and into the redeemed life. When we answer the call, God sends us into new life, a life where we give ourselves over to ways that are beyond our imagining.

Like Isaiah, we need to be open to God's call, to respond by saying, "Here I am." But "here I am" is just the beginning. God's call is always a call to action, to *go*, to move as an actor in bringing God's call to life. It is why our worship concludes with prayers that "send us out to do the work you have given us to do, as faithful witnesses of Christ our Lord." Our response is not simply to acknowledge God's call but to act on it. Here I am; send me. I will go.

The Rev. Dr. Bill Lupfer
Rector
Trinity Church Wall Street
New York City, New York

Questions

What do you think God's response would be today if you said, "Here I am. Send me!" How would your life be changed?

What does it mean for you to be "sent" by God? What role do you see for yourself in spreading the good news?

Prayer

Everliving God, whose will it is that all should come to you through your Son Jesus Christ: Inspire our witness to him, that all may know the power of his forgiveness and the hope of his resurrection; who lives and reigns with you and the Holy Spirit, one God, now and for ever. *Amen.*

—*The Book of Common Prayer*, p. 816

Matthew 28:5-10

[5]But the angel said to the women, "Do not be afraid; I know that you are looking for Jesus who was crucified. [6]He is not here; for he has been raised, as he said. Come, see the place where he lay. [7]Then go quickly and tell his disciples, 'He has been raised from the dead, and indeed he is going ahead of you to Galilee; there you will see him.' This is my message for you." [8]So they left the tomb quickly with fear and great joy, and ran to tell his disciples. [9]Suddenly Jesus met them and said, "Greetings!" And they came to him, took hold of his feet, and worshiped him. [10]Then Jesus said to them, "Do not be afraid; go and tell my brothers to go to Galilee; there they will see me."

Reflection

I had a professor who explained that the audible voice of God came to her and shook the rafters as he told her, "TEACH!" This is how I understood calling, waiting patiently upon the Lord to break my ceiling—or at least shake a tile loose. Over the years, I hoped for the same clarity of purpose, the same certainty, the same pursuit of a singularly achievable task.

I still listen for that call—daily, even. In the meantime, I have spent most of my adult life jumping from place to place, eager to start a new adventure or try a new thing. Over the last fifteen years, I have found home in Michigan, Virginia, Tennessee, Minnesota, and New York. I have found the ones I love in each of these places—the brilliant and the caring, the good and the funny, the melancholy, the joyful, and the kind of people who defy any kind of categorization. And when the time has come to move to the next exciting thing, I mope around for weeks, unsure of whether the next place will hold the same goodness as the last. Just like the women at the tomb, there is fear and great joy every time we go anywhere.

Presiding Bishop Michael Curry once explained that for Christians, Galilee is shorthand for the wider world. Jesus has gone ahead of us into the cities, the fields, the hospitals, the villages, and more. Perhaps, then, the call for all of us is to Go—to find where he has already gone ahead, to meet anew the people he knows and loves there, to embrace the fear and great joy.

"Go to Galilee; there they will see me," he promises.

Christopher Sikkema
Manager for Special Projects
The Episcopal Church
Rochester, Minnesota

Questions

Where have you gone with fear and great joy? Where would you like to go?

Where is Galilee for you? Is it somewhere you know well? Somewhere far away?

Prayer

O God, our heavenly Father, whose glory fills the whole creation, and whose presence we find wherever we go: Preserve those who travel; surround them with your loving care; protect them from every danger; and bring them in safety to their journey's end; through Jesus Christ our Lord. *Amen.*

—*The Book of Common Prayer*, p. 831

Luke 10:25-37

[25]Just then a lawyer stood up to test Jesus. "Teacher," he said, "what must I do to inherit eternal life?" [26]He said to him, "What is written in the law? What do you read there?" [27]He answered, "You shall love the Lord your God with all your heart, and with all your soul, and with all your strength, and with all your mind; and your neighbor as yourself." [28]And he said to him, "You have given the right answer; do this, and you will live."

[29]But wanting to justify himself, he asked Jesus, "And who is my neighbor?" [30]Jesus replied, "A man was going down from Jerusalem to Jericho, and fell into the hands of robbers, who stripped him, beat him, and went away, leaving him half dead. [31]Now by chance a priest was going down that road; and when he saw him, he passed by on the other side. [32]So likewise a Levite, when he came to the place and saw him, passed by on the other side. [33]But a Samaritan while traveling came near him; and when he saw him, he was moved with pity. [34]He went to him and bandaged his wounds, having poured oil and wine on them. Then he put him on his own animal, brought him to an inn, and took care of him. [35]The next day he took out two denarii, gave them to the innkeeper, and said, 'Take care of him; and when I come back, I will repay you whatever more you spend.' [36]Which of these three, do you think, was a neighbor to the man who fell into the hands of the robbers?" [37]He said, "The one who showed him mercy." Jesus said to him, "Go and do likewise."

Reflection

Some Christians are centered in their heads and others in their hearts. Some are contemplatives, and others are action oriented. In the parable of the Good Samaritan, a lawyer who appears as someone whose religion is compartmentalized in his head puts Jesus to the test: "Teacher, what must I do to inherit eternal life?"

The Pharisees in Jesus' time believe there is a life after death. Some believe the dead descend into a nether world that is like a great banquet hall filled with friends and family who have preceded us in death, sitting around tables filled with lavish food and drink, awaiting us. Others believe the dead remain in their tombs until they are raised from the dead along with the Messiah.

Jesus meets the lawyer on his own terms. "What is written in the law?" asks Jesus. The lawyer recites the two great love commandments, whereby Jesus innovatively links our love for God with love for our neighbor. Jesus applauds his answer. But wanting to justify himself, the lawyer requests a definition of what is a neighbor. It sounds like the modern equivalent in congregations: Who is a church member?

Like a good rabbi, Jesus tells a story, one of the greatest stories in the Bible. It takes place between Jerusalem and Jericho, which are sixteen miles apart. The road drops precipitously from Jerusalem, located 3,800 feet above sea level, and Jericho, which is 840 feet above sea level.

In between is a remote stretch called the Bloody Way, where bandits hide behind boulders waiting to ambush, rob, and beat unsuspecting travelers. The star of this story is a Samaritan, whose faith is an offshoot of Judaism that only accepts the first five books of the

Hebrew scriptures. Jews scorn Samaritans, but Jesus elevates one as a hero.

Jesus asks his inquisitor, "Which of these three, do you think, was a neighbor to the man who fell into the hands of robbers?" The lawyer answers, "The one who showed him mercy." Jesus says, "Go and do likewise." In Luke's Gospel, Jesus frequently says, "Go." Go in peace. Get up and go on your way. Christianity is an action religion. We are asked to mobilize our faith, to allow our faith to descend from our head to our heart. Christianity is always a balance between contemplation and action, worship and service, listening and doing.

The Rev. Marek P. Zabriskie
Founder, The Bible Challenge
Rector, Christ Church
Greenwich, Connecticut

Questions

Are you more at ease with doing something for God or sitting in God's presence receiving inspiration and being filled by the Spirit?

Do you have or lack a balance in your spiritual life between action and contemplation? Does your faith gravitate to the head or to the heart?

Prayer

Holy and gracious God, you call us to be transformed and then deploy us in action to care for the profound needs of the world and to help people who have been beaten down by adversity, suffering, misfortune, and poverty. Help us to see our neighbors not as threats but as opportunities for serving you by caring for those in need as we reach out and respond; to get up and go once we have heard you call our name and invite us into your loving service. *Amen.*

Rest

John 14:15-31

¹⁵"If you love me, you will keep my commandments. ¹⁶And I will ask the Father, and he will give you another Advocate, to be with you forever. ¹⁷This is the Spirit of truth, whom the world cannot receive, because it neither sees him nor knows him. You know him, because he abides with you, and he will be in you.

¹⁸"I will not leave you orphaned; I am coming to you. ¹⁹In a little while the world will no longer see me, but you will see me; because I live, you also will live. ²⁰On that day you will know that I am in my Father, and you in me, and I in you. ²¹They who have my commandments and keep them are those who love me; and those who love me will be loved by my Father, and I will love them and reveal myself to them." ²²Judas (not Iscariot) said to him, "Lord, how is it that you will reveal yourself to us, and not to the world?" ²³Jesus answered him, "Those who love me will keep my word, and my Father will love them, and we will come to them and make our home with them. ²⁴Whoever does not love me does not keep my words; and the word that you hear is not mine, but is from the Father who sent me.

²⁵"I have said these things to you while I am still with you. ²⁶But the Advocate, the Holy Spirit, whom the Father will send in my name, will teach you everything, and remind you of all that I have said to you. ²⁷Peace I leave with you; my peace I give to you. I do not give to you as the world gives. Do not let your hearts be troubled, and do not let them be afraid. ²⁸You heard me say to you, 'I am going away, and I am coming to you.' If you loved me, you would rejoice that I am going to the Father, because the

Father is greater than I. [29]And now I have told you this before it occurs, so that when it does occur, you may believe. [30]I will no longer talk much with you, for the ruler of this world is coming. He has no power over me; [31]but I do as the Father has commanded me, so that the world may know that I love the Father. Rise, let us be on our way."

Reflection

Some years ago, after undergoing minor surgery, I was told by my doctor that I needed to take it easy for three days. Something about the way he spoke to me let me know this was more than a suggestion, so I took him seriously. Two days later, sitting in my study reading a book, I suddenly realized this was the first time in a long time that I had given myself permission to really rest. How tragic, I thought, that I literally had to be cut open before I could find rest.

We all seem to have so much to do these days. And while our cell phones, computers, and tablets are supposed to make our lives more efficient, they also keep us constantly available, plugged-in, and on call. Real moments of rest—when we slow down, unplug, and have time to reflect—seem harder to come by. But if life can only be lived while moving forward, it can only be understood by taking time to look back and process what has already taken place. We need rest to be able to take stock of our lives, to detect God's presence in our lives, and to find direction for our lives. When we take time to rest, we take time to find peace, to gain perspective, to garner insight, and to re-create ourselves so that we can live more fully.

I pray you will have enough time to forget about time. I pray you will find the space to live in the moment. I pray you will find the silence to hear how much God loves you. I pray you will be able to calm your soul enough to see the immense beauty in every blade of grass and in every grain of sand. I pray that you will make room in your life to read and dream, to eat well and sleep soundly. Carving out significant time for rest is not a luxury; it is crucial to the well-being of our souls.

The Very Rev. Randolph Marshall Hollerith
Dean
Washington National Cathedral
Washington, D.C.

The Way of Love

Questions

How much time each week do you take for rest and reflection, time when you are not asleep? Is it enough?

What three things worry you the most? What would it take for you to be able to put these worries aside for a few hours and rest?

When have you felt most at peace? What was going on in your life during those moments? How can you create new moments in your life to experience that peace once again?

Prayer

Be present, O merciful God, and protect us through the hours of this night, so that we who are wearied by the changes and chances of this life may rest in your eternal changelessness; through Jesus Christ our Lord. *Amen.*

—*The Book of Common Prayer*, p. 133

Psalm 127:1-2

1   Unless the LORD builds the house, *
       their labor is in vain who build it.

2   Unless the LORD watches over the city, *
       in vain the watchman keeps his vigil.

The Way of Love

Reflection

Some years ago, someone mentioned workaholism, and I foolishly sought a definition. My Sisters started laughing! I was stunned. So what if I got up extra early and headed straight for my desk? So what if I was multitasking during worship, planning, quietly jotting notes? Isn't that what one does? Use God's gift of time efficiently?

Older now, and hopefully wiser, I still need to learn. How do I know *God* is asking me to do everything I'm doing? Take writing these meditations. When the invitation came to contribute, I didn't pause for a moment before accepting. Response to a call? Ego? What if I had stopped to listen, to rest in the question first? Maybe I would be writing this. Or not. Maybe God had someone else in mind.

Unless the Lord builds the house…Unless the Lord guards the city…It is in vain… As I write around this theme, seeking my way, we are in silent retreat. I chose to do this today, literally to rest in these difficult (for me) verses. Another day will be set aside for editing, pruning, fixing. Today is for resting, listening for the quiet whisper of the Spirit, free writing as my heart struggles to be open, letting the questions flow, letting them go and drifting off into a nap.

A new translation of the Hebrew text has the final line of Psalm 127: 2 as "So much he gives to his loved ones in sleep." What if it's not just a matter of our bodies receiving necessary sleep to keep functioning but there's something else God wants to give us while we sleep, while our guard is down, while we are not too busy to receive it? May we rest and receive and let go and trust.

The Rev. Sr. Diana Dorothea Doncaster, CT
Sister and Priest
Community of the Transfiguration
Glendale, Ohio

Questions

If you deal with workaholism, how does it affect your ability to be present with God in prayer and worship?

How do you decide whether or not to take on a new responsibility? Does your need for rest and renewal figure into your thinking and praying?

Prayer

O God of Sabbath, thank you for sacred gifts you give through rest and sleep. Help me to entrust to you what I do not accomplish, to distinguish the truly important from my desire to feel important; for you, not work, are the Way, the Truth, and the Life. *Amen.*

Matthew 11:25-30

[25]At that time Jesus said, "I thank you, Father, Lord of heaven and earth, because you have hidden these things from the wise and the intelligent and have revealed them to infants; [26]yes, Father, for such was your gracious will. [27]All things have been handed over to me by my Father; and no one knows the Son except the Father, and no one knows the Father except the Son and anyone to whom the Son chooses to reveal him.

[28]"Come to me, all you that are weary and are carrying heavy burdens, and I will give you rest. [29]Take my yoke upon you, and learn from me; for I am gentle and humble in heart, and you will find rest for your souls. [30]For my yoke is easy, and my burden is light."

Reflection

Many people increasingly describe themselves as living in a state of permanent overload and exhaustion. Multitasking to optimize productivity has only worsened our sense of malaise, making rest one of the most desperately needed natural resources of our time.

In part we crave physical rest, but Jesus seems to be speaking here to a deeper deficit, a soul-weariness. He calls the antidote he offers "hidden" knowledge, not because it is esoteric but because it is overlooked, something children might find obvious but those of us who live in our heads may not.

What Jesus offers is not freedom from stress but rather a different way of carrying our burdens, one that is enigmatically "easy" and "light." Nearly all the healing stories of Jesus show him saying in a dozen different ways: *Why are you still carrying that burden? Drop it. Stand up. See. Hear. Know forgiveness. Go free.*

Jesus' understanding of rest is anchored in the sabbath—a literal, periodic shutdown and cessation from normal duties in order to renew and restore depleted bodies and spirits. That is a nonnegotiable for any generative way of life. But there is a further dimension of soul-sabbath Jesus points to, one that could, in the words of preacher-poet George Herbert, last "seven whole days, not one in seven."

Jesus describes the source of his rest as being "gentle and humble in heart." It's clear as one reads through the Jesus stories that gentle does not mean docile but rather points to Jesus' courageous kindness and inclusive reach. Humble means being so radically grounded that even humiliation cannot touch him.

Rooting in the present moment and being courageously kind brings a centeredness that vastly expands the concept of rest. So much of the weight of our lives turns out to be self-generated, with all the extra drama and attachments we add. Imagine adding nothing extra to life's weight; let the burden be light!

The Rev. Daniel Simons
Director of Spiritual Formation
Trinity Retreat Center
West Cornwall, Connecticut

Questions

Take a few minutes to do a brief scan of your life. Where are the places that most deeply restore you? And the places that deplete you? Just notice them, and see what next action suggests itself. Imagine Jesus coming up to you and saying, "Stand up to your full height, and just let it go!" What would he be talking about?

On one of your days off, turn off your devices and reduce or eliminate errands. Watch how the time expands. How could you make this a regular practice?

Prayer

O God, our hearts are restless until they find their rest in you. Bring us to that place of abiding in you where we know ourselves to be forgiven, loved, and free; give us the courage to be kind, and the groundedness to discern justice, as we follow the light footsteps of Jesus, in whose Name we pray. *Amen.*

Psalm 23

1   The LORD is my shepherd; *
        I shall not be in want.

2   He makes me lie down in green pastures *
        and leads me beside still waters.

3   He revives my soul *
        and guides me along right pathways for his Name's sake.

4   Though I walk through the valley of the shadow of death,
    I shall fear no evil; *
        for you are with me;
        your rod and your staff, they comfort me.

5   You spread a table before me in the presence of those who
                trouble me; *
        you have anointed my head with oil,
        and my cup is running over.

6   Surely your goodness and mercy shall follow me all the days
                of my life, *
        and I will dwell in the house of the LORD for ever.

Reflection

The pain had been so horrific that by the time I returned home after emergency spinal surgery, I felt pretty good in contrast. In fact, by about day ten, I figured I was ready to go back to the office. Just for a few hours. I had a lot of work to do—important stuff that I determined couldn't wait. My boss didn't pressure me. My colleagues were surprised to see me. There was no real reason why I was back to work except for my own sense of duty—and perhaps self-importance.

When I went to the neurosurgeon for my first check-up, I asked when I could return to work full time. (I had already been part time for two weeks). He responded sternly that we would discuss a slow return to work at my three-month appointment. But I pushed through, figuring my body would simply heal while I continued on my merry way.

Turns out, rest is critical. I discovered this lesson on Christmas morning when I couldn't get out of bed or walk or shower without assistance. Surgery fixed the immediate injury, but the muscles and nerves needed time. They needed rest.

Occasionally I can better understand puzzling pieces of scripture when I view them through the lens of God taking care of God's people. The edict against eating pork? God didn't want people to suffer from trichinosis. Declaring a woman who had just given birth unclean? Perhaps the semi-isolation protected the new mother and child from germs and allowed time to bond.

I had always struggled to understand God's requirement for us to rest, to honor the sabbath. Didn't God value industriousness and a commitment to hard work? God has many reasons, I'm sure, for calling us to rest, but I have come to believe one of the purposes is God's desire to take care of us. God knows what we need—spiritually, emotionally, physically—when we cannot understand or will not accept it ourselves. The prophet Isaiah says there's no rest for the wicked, but our loving God offers rest, requires it even, for God's holy children, for you, for me, and for all the worried and wearied.

Richelle Thompson
Deputy Director and Managing Editor
Forward Movement
Fort Thomas, Kentucky

Questions

It's one thing to ignore doctor's orders. But how often do you ignore God's directive to rest? Spend some time in deep reflection, asking yourself to honestly name the things keeping you from rest.

How can a practice of rest support the other spiritual practices of the Way of Love?

Prayer

For health and strength to work, and leisure to rest and play, we thank you, Lord. *Amen.*

—*The Book of Common Prayer*, p. 837

Isaiah 58:13-14

¹³If you refrain from trampling the sabbath, from pursuing your own interests on my holy day; if you call the sabbath a delight and the holy day of the Lord honorable; if you honor it, not going your own ways, serving your own interests, or pursuing your own affairs; ¹⁴then you shall take delight in the Lord, and I will make you ride upon the heights of the earth; I will feed you with the heritage of your ancestor Jacob, for the mouth of the Lord has spoken.

Reflection

The Way of Love practice that I have the hardest time following is rest. I'm not talking about the rest of taking a nap or binge-watching my favorite show, but the true, restorative rest that God demands we offer one day a week, where we devote time to spiritual pursuits. Laundry, I guarantee you, is not a spiritual pursuit, no matter how you try to dress it up. Remembering the sabbath is the fourth commandment—and the only commandment that I believe we break consistently and with pride.

Our culture is in a place where we honor busyness. We celebrate our overcommitted schedules, our burgeoning calendars, our inability to get everything done. We pack ourselves tight along with our children and our parents and call it a life well lived. Following the Way of Love reminds us that there is a different path we can take. Isaiah makes clear what happens when we follow our own interests and pursue our own affairs: We trample the sabbath, and we do not honor God with our actions.

With my feet firmly planted in midlife, with aging children on one side and aging and dying parents on the other, I need to acknowledge that rest is what God demands of me—of all of us—and what we must demand of ourselves. No matter how significant our work, no matter how important our child's dance practice, no matter how serious our parent's doctor's visit, we must restore our hearts and minds so that we can live fully into a God-filled existence.

When we genuinely rest, we do as God does. When we rest, we give ourselves time to follow all of the other practices of the Way of Love.

As these are daily practices, we should allocate some time every day for restoration. On our sabbath day, we should aspire to give the entire day to God. As long as we're doing something as radical as following Jesus, why not go even further and do whatever it takes to have a holy sabbath?

Miriam Willard McKenney
Development Director
Forward Movement
Cincinnati, Ohio

Questions

What prevents you from honoring the sabbath? What activities or chores take place on the sabbath that you could do on another day? Take inventory of your calendar and schedule those activities on another day of the week.

Who do you need to help you get more rest and honor God's day? Look to the people in your life—your children (no matter their ages), parents, loved ones, and co-workers—and ask for help to clear that path to a holy sabbath.

Prayer

O God, in the course of this busy life, give us times of refreshment and peace; and grant that we may so use our leisure to rebuild our bodies and renew our minds, that our spirits may be opened to the goodness of your creation; through Jesus Christ our Lord. *Amen.*

—*The Book of Common Prayer*, p. 825

The Way of Love

Exodus 20:8-11

[8]Remember the sabbath day, and keep it holy. [9]Six days you shall labor and do all your work. [10]But the seventh day is a sabbath to the LORD your God; you shall not do any work—you, your son or your daughter, your male or female slave, your livestock, or the alien resident in your towns.

[11]For in six days the LORD made heaven and earth, the sea, and all that is in them, but rested the seventh day; therefore the LORD blessed the sabbath day and consecrated it.

Reflection

I have served as a Christian educator in the Episcopal Church for nearly thirty years. The idea of Sunday, the seventh day, being a day of rest, is laughable. Yes, I often squeeze in an afternoon nap, but for all intents and purposes, it is a work day.

In November of 2017, I experienced an acute episode of anxiety and panic attacks. Being open about my mental illness has been life-giving for me. There is still a significant stigma associated with mental illness, but thankfully, things seem to be changing. I am not afraid to share my story.

For a period of about six weeks, I did not sleep, and I did not eat. I lost thirty pounds in three weeks. I felt like I was going crazy. I would cry for hours—sometimes for days. My family was scared. I was scared. I ended up in the emergency room twice. I thought I was dying.

Then it was given a name. I, Roger Hutchison, the artist, author, Christian educator, husband, parent, always smiling, always happy-go-lucky fella was diagnosed with generalized anxiety disorder. Generalized anxiety disorder (GAD) is characterized by persistent and excessive worry about a number of different things. People with GAD may anticipate disaster and may be overly concerned about money, health, family, work, or other issues. I was exhausted, broken, and at rock bottom. It took some time and a lot of personal work, but things improved. I am grateful for my family, colleagues, friends, therapist, and psychiatrist for my recovery.

Being diagnosed with a mental illness is one of the best things that has ever happened to me. Seriously. We are running our hearts, minds, and bodies into the ground. We worship at the altar of busyness, and we are losing.

Sunday is not a day of rest for me. I have learned, though, to take sabbath time every day. I begin and end my day with meditation. I practice deep breathing throughout the day. I spend time with the scriptures. I read and write poetry. I paint pictures. "And the Lord blessed and consecrated it."

Roger Hutchison
Director of Christian Formation and Parish Life
Palmer Memorial Episcopal Church
Houston, Texas

Questions

Are you an anxious person? If so, how do you manage your anxiety?

How do you honor and keep sabbath time in your life? If you have a difficult time doing this, what small step might you take to make this a priority?

Prayer

O God of peace, who hast taught us that in returning and rest we shall be saved, in quietness and in confidence shall be our strength: By the might of thy Spirit lift us, we pray thee, to thy presence, where we may be still and know that thou art God; through Jesus Christ our Lord. *Amen.*

—*The Book of Common Prayer*, p. 832

Hebrews 4:1-16

¹Therefore, while the promise of entering his rest is still open, let us take care that none of you should seem to have failed to reach it. ²For indeed the good news came to us just as to them; but the message they heard did not benefit them, because they were not united by faith with those who listened. ³For we who have believed enter that rest, just as God has said, "As in my anger I swore, 'They shall not enter my rest,'" though his works were finished at the foundation of the world. ⁴For in one place it speaks about the seventh day as follows, "And God rested on the seventh day from all his works." ⁵And again in this place it says, "They shall not enter my rest." ⁶Since therefore it remains open for some to enter it, and those who formerly received the good news failed to enter because of disobedience, ⁷again he sets a certain day—"today"—saying through David much later, in the words already quoted, "Today, if you hear his voice, do not harden your hearts." ⁸For if Joshua had given them rest, God would not speak later about another day. ⁹So then, a sabbath rest still remains for the people of God; ¹⁰for those who enter God's rest also cease from their labors as God did from his. ¹¹Let us therefore make every effort to enter that rest, so that no one may fall through such disobedience as theirs.

¹²Indeed, the word of God is living and active, sharper than any two-edged sword, piercing until it divides soul from spirit, joints from marrow; it is able to judge the thoughts and intentions of the heart. ¹³And before him no creature is hidden, but all are naked and laid bare to

the eyes of the one to whom we must render an account.

[14]Since, then, we have a great high priest who has passed through the heavens, Jesus, the Son of God, let us hold fast to our confession. [15]For we do not have a high priest who is unable to sympathize with our weaknesses, but we have one who in every respect has been tested as we are, yet without sin. [16]Let us therefore approach the throne of grace with boldness, so that we may receive mercy and find grace to help in time of need.

Reflection

A normal resting heart rate for adults ranges from 60 to 100 beats per minute. Many factors can influence heart rate, including age, fitness, emotions, medications, and more.

But what about a "resting soul rate?" What would that look like? What if we could measure our souls' rest?

Medical science tells us that our bodies need rest in order to thrive, and this passage from Hebrews tells us that to thrive in the Christian life, we need rest—and not physical rest but soul rest, God's rest.

So, how does God rest? According to Genesis 2, God looks back at what has been done, calls it good, blesses the work, and then pauses for restoration, ceasing from all productivity.

Noticing. Appreciating. Blessing. Pausing. Restorating. Savoring. These are the markers of what God's rest looks like. Are they the markers of our practice of rest? If not, what are the consequences?

When I am bone tired, in body and soul, I am less likely to have the margin to notice the beauty around me. When I am frazzled and worn down, what are the chances I will be able to see all that I have accomplished over the week and call it good instead of what I usually call it: not enough?

Like sleep-deprived toddlers unable to choose between chicken nuggets and a grilled cheese sandwich, when our bodies and our souls are not rested, we are often reduced to our least-healthy selves. We are more likely to be snappy, impatient, ungrateful, and unwelcoming.

We are disobedient to the commandment to love our neighbor as ourselves, disobedient to the charges to be patient, generous, long-suffering, forgiving, and humble.

My prayer is that we can begin to see rest as an act of obedience instead of weakness, that we will make time to practice noticing, appreciating, blessing, pausing, restoring, and savoring so that we might live healthy lives as Christ followers.

Jerusalem Greer
Staff Officer for Evangelism
The Episcopal Church
Greenbrier, Arkansas

Questions

What tiny practice of rest can you begin today in order to establish a healthy "resting soul rate?" Maybe observe ten minutes of silence each day? A daily media-free hour?

What unhealthy behaviors do you act out when your soul is not rested? How can you begin to make space to notice, appreciate, and celebrate all that you accomplish each week, calling it good?

Prayer

Gracious God, you created rest so we might find our way back to you and to ourselves. Guide us in our practice. Gently nudge us to call our labors good instead of not enough. Help us to value rest as a gift and not just a means to an end. Thank you for setting before us the ability to choose between life and death, and may we choose life again and again. *Amen.*

Matthew 28:16-20

¹⁶Now the eleven disciples went to Galilee, to the mountain to which Jesus had directed them. ¹⁷When they saw him, they worshiped him; but some doubted. ¹⁸And Jesus came and said to them, "All authority in heaven and on earth has been given to me. ¹⁹Go therefore and make disciples of all nations, baptizing them in the name of the Father and of the Son and of the Holy Spirit, ²⁰and teaching them to obey everything that I have commanded you. And remember, I am with you always, to the end of the age."

Reflection

A gun show forced us to take the leap of faith. Our church plant had been meeting for worship at a small community center. We transported the processional cross and candles in a "holy" golf bag and the liturgical accoutrements in a plastic tote. The setup wasn't fancy, but new folks came each week, and our worship was authentic and heartfelt.

But the township made a scheduling error, and one Sunday we showed up to transform the space for Holy Eucharist and found vendors setting up a gun show. Earlier in the week, the fledgling congregation had purchased land that included a 150-year-old house and a rundown pole barn, the location for our future church home after at least a year of renovation and construction.

Instead, we moved to the land that Sunday morning and held the service of Holy Eucharist under the shade of an old oak tree. For three months, we sat in folding chairs on the side lawn, singing hymns, breaking bread, and praising God. Amazingly (miraculously, even, for the Midwest), not a drop of rain fell on those Sundays from 10 a.m. to noon. Not once in those three months.

This Way of Love is a leap of faith. It is believing that when we seek not our own way but God's way, God will provide. When we turn to God and away from our own expectations and desires, we discover that the shade of a tree and the promise of blue skies is sanctuary enough. When we read and learn God's Word, when we pray and worship together, we experience God in the rustle of leaves and car horns honking as they pass by a makeshift church.

When we practice both being a blessing to others and graciously receiving blessings, we glorify God by seeing opportunity in the midst of challenge. When we go, we take risks for Jesus' sake and find him with us and before us. And when we rest—when we finally, gratefully rest—God renews our spirit, reinvigorating us to go out once again to see and seek Christ in others and to be the Way of Love for all.

Richelle Thompson
Deputy Director and Managing Editor
Forward Movement
Fort Thomas, Kentucky

Question _____

Which spiritual practice of the Way of Love appeals most to you? Which one needs the most practice? Have you considered writing a Rule of Life that could help you to consciously and consistently embrace these spiritual practices?

Close your eyes for a minute and dream an answer to this question: How might the Way of Love transform the world? Now, open your eyes and take your next steps in living the Way of Love.

Prayer _____

O gracious Lord, we pray that we, being rooted and established in love, may have power, together with all the Lord's holy people, to grasp how wide and long and high and deep is the love of Christ, and to know this love that surpasses knowledge, that we may be filled to the measure of all the fullness of God. *Amen.*

About the Contributors

BILL CAMPBELL is the executive director of Forma, which is the Network for Christian Formation. He has more than fifteen years of experience as a lay leader in the Episcopal Church. Having served as a youth minister, children's minister, and adult educator as well as a fundraiser, Bill is excited to continue his ministry with Forma. Bill's passion is finding ways for churches, dioceses, and organizations to collaborate. *Pages 54, 107*

MEGAN L. CASTELLAN is the rector of St. John's Episcopal Church in Ithaca, New York. She has written for outlets as diverse as *Episcopal Café, Lent Madness, McSweeney's Internet Tendency*, and *The* (late, lamented) *Toast*, as well as contributed to several published books from Church Publishing. When not writing, she enjoys watching her husband play video games and watching her pets plan world domination. *Pages 124, 131*

BARBARA CAWTHORNE CRAFTON is an Episcopal priest and author. Retired from parish ministry, Barbara writes books and conducts occasional retreats. Her *Almost-Daily eMos* from the Geranium Farm, read online for years by thousands worldwide, are archived on the Farm, www.geraniumfarm.org. She and her husband, retired English professor Richard Quaintance, are newly settled in Boulder, Colorado. *Pages 63, 142*

DIANA DOROTHEA DONCASTER, CT is a Sister of the Community of the Transfiguration, an Episcopal order for women in Cincinnati, Ohio. She was ordained a priest in 2015. Her ministries include writing nonfiction, fiction, and hymns. She serves as a spiritual companion, a supply priest, liturgist, dishwasher, wheelchair pusher, and servant to the most delightful cat in the world. *Pages 66, 167*

JENIFER GAMBER serves as assistant rector and chaplain to the Day School at St. Patrick's Episcopal Church in Washington, D.C. She is a trusted retreat leader and author of several books, including *My Faith, My Life: A Teen's Guide to the Episcopal Church* and *Call on Me: A Prayer Book for Young People*. Jenifer serves on the Way of Love leadership group for the Episcopal Church and finds joy in liturgy and Christian formation. *Pages 85, 88, 127*

JERUSALEM GREER is a staff officer for evangelism for the Episcopal Church. She is also the author of the books *A Homemade Year* and *At Home in this Life*. She lives with her family on a hobby farm in central Arkansas. *Pages 102, 187*

RANDOLPH MARSHALL HOLLERITH began his tenure as the eleventh dean of Washington National Cathedral in 2016. Prior to his call to the cathedral, Randy served as rector of St. James's Episcopal Church in Richmond, Virginia, rector of St. Peter's Episcopal Church in Savannah, Georgia, and as assistant rector of St. Stephen's Episcopal Church in Richmond, Virginia. *Pages 145, 164*

BRENDA HUSSON is a graduate of Union Theological Seminary. Ordained by the Diocese of Central New York, Brenda's entire ministry has been spent in the Diocese of New York. She has served four parishes of very different sizes in three counties. She is currently in her twenty-third year as rector at St. James' Church in Manhattan. She is married to Tom Faulkner, an Episcopal priest and professional sculptor. They are the proud parents of a son, Christopher. *Page 117*

ROGER HUTCHISON is the director of Christian formation and parish life at Palmer Memorial Episcopal Church in Houston, Texas, and author of *The Painting Table: A Journal of Loss and Joy*. He had the privilege of painting with children who had experienced the tragic shootings at Sandy Hook Elementary in Newtown, Connecticut. The experience affected him profoundly and convinced him of a vocation to use his writing and art to serve those who grieve. *Pages 51, 182*

PHILLIP A. JACKSON has served parishes in Houston, Detroit, and Phoenix; he is currently the vicar of Trinity Church Wall Street. In this role, he oversees the parish Congregational Council, a body of laypeople who help envision and coordinate the ministries of the parish. It has been his great pleasure these past four years in seeing this group of talented and committed Christians blossom with exciting and outward-focused ministry. *Page 31*

LISA KIMBALL is the associate dean of lifelong learning and professor of Christian formation and congregational leadership at Virginia Theological Seminary. She was privileged to participate in the creation of *The Way of Love: Practices for Jesus-Centered Life*. She is currently directing *Baptized for Life: An Episcopal Discipleship Initiative* using the discipleship process of the ancient catechumenate to prepare people to claim their Christian calling with joy and confidence. *Page 36*

FRANK S. LOGUE serves as the canon to the ordinary of the Diocese of Georgia, assisting the bishop in forming persons for ministry, discerning the right fit between clergy and congregations, and supporting the discipleship and numeric growth of the congregations of the diocese. He previously served as the church planter for King of Peace Episcopal Church in Kingsland, Georgia. He is a member of the Executive Council of the Episcopal Church. *Pages 18, 80*

WILLIAM LUPFER is the eighteenth rector of Trinity Church Wall Street in New York City, a role he has held since 2015. He leads Trinity's efforts to build neighborhoods that live Trinity's core values, generations of faithful leadership, and financial capacity in service to New York City and around the world. Before joining Trinity, he was dean of Trinity Episcopal Cathedral in Portland, Oregon, and served in parishes in Detroit and Chicago. He holds a master of divinity degree from Yale Divinity School and received his doctorate of ministry from Seabury-Western Theological Seminary. He has been married to Kimiko Koga Lupfer for twenty-eight years. They have two children. *Pages 5, 151*

SHANNON MACVEAN-BROWN is the interim rector of St. Thomas Church in Franklin, Indiana. She is a priest, artist, educator, wife, and mother who has a passion for working with communities of faith to build their understanding of the Baptismal Covenant and how it draws us to be present in our communities, no matter our location. She is dedicated to social justice work in the church and the community, as seen in her service on the Episcopal Church Taskforce on Women, Justice, and Reconciliation, ACT Indiana, and as president of Faith in Indiana. Her artistry can be seen in the liturgies she creates, her poetry and icon writing, and in other creative endeavors that nourish her spirituality, such as sermon writing, which she views as an act of prayer and discernment. *Pages 74, 148*

ANDREW MCGOWAN is dean and president of Berkeley Divinity School at Yale and teaches Anglican studies and Ancient Christianity there. An Australian, he was previously warden and president of Trinity College, The University of Melbourne. His most recent book is *Ancient Christian Worship*. *Pages 22, 98*

Miriam Willard McKenney loves her family fiercely. She serves as development director at Forward Movement where she works to increase the ministry to provide resources to anyone in need. Miriam also serves as youth minister at Calvary Episcopal Church in Cincinnati with the children she led in Godly Play. *Pages 15, 178*

Sara Miles is the author of *Take This Bread: A Radical Conversion* and *City of God: Faith in the Streets.* She served as director of ministry for ten years at St. Gregory of Nyssa Episcopal Church in San Francisco and is the founder of The Food Pantry there. She lives in San Francisco and currently works as accompaniment coordinator with Faith in Action Bay Area and speaks and preaches around the country. *Pages 9, 92*

Sandra T. Montes was born in Perú and is an independent consultant and musician. She grew up in Guatemala and settled in Texas as soon as she could. Sandra has been developing original bilingual resources, volunteering, and working in the Episcopal Church and serves as musician, translator, speaker, consultant, and writer. She earned her doctorate in education in 2016 and is a full-time independent consultant and musician as well as works part-time with the Episcopal Church Foundation as its consultant for Spanish language resources. *Pages 77, 134*

Mary Foster Parmer is the creator of the ministry of Invite Welcome Connect, and she currently serves as the director of Invite Welcome Connect at the Beecken Center of the School of Theology, University of the South in Sewanee, Tennessee. Mary is the past director of the Gathering of Leaders, a national leadership gathering of young Episcopal clergy. Mary holds a degree in religious studies from St. Edwards University in Austin and formerly served as director of adult ministries and evangelism at St. Stephen's, Beaumont, Texas. *Pages 26, 121*

C. K. ROBERTSON is canon to the presiding bishop for ministry beyond the Episcopal Church and distinguished visiting professor at The General Theological Seminary. A member of the Council on Foreign Relations and vice president of the board of *The Anglican Theological Review*, Chuck serves as general editor of the *Studies in Episcopal & Anglican Theology* series and has written more than a dozen books, including *Barnabas vs. Paul*. *Pages 12, 47*

CHRISTOPHER SIKKEMA serves as the manager for special projects in the Office of Communication for the Episcopal Church, working with the Way of Love, Becoming Beloved Community, Episcopal Revivals, Sermons That Work, and the Episcopal Asset Map. He is currently based from Rochester, Minnesota. He earned a bachelor's degree in political science and religion from Hope College in Holland, Michigan, and a master's degree in theology, focusing on the history of religion in America, from Vanderbilt University in Nashville, Tennessee. Before his current role, he served with Jubilee Ministries of the Episcopal Church and studied Appalachian serpent handling and the Catholic Movement in the nineteenth-century Episcopal Church. *Pages 95, 154*

DANIEL SIMONS is an Episcopal priest currently serving as director of spiritual formation at the Trinity Retreat Center in West Cornwall, Connecticut, a ministry of Trinity Church Wall Street in New York City, where he had served for the past ten years. He brings to the retreat center more than twenty-five years of specialized ministry in spiritual formation, intentional community, and pilgrimage. *Pages 70, 170*

Becca Stevens is an author, priest, and founder and president of Thistle Farms, a global community of survivors of trafficking and addiction that includes justice enterprises. For her work as an entrepreneur and justice advocate, Becca was named a White House Champion of Change and a CNN Hero, and holds numerous honorary doctorates. She has been featured on *The Today Show*, *ABC World News*, *NPR*, and in *The New York Times*. Her most recent book is *Love Heals*. *Page 113*

Richelle Thompson serves as managing editor and deputy director of Forward Movement. She lives with her husband and their two teenagers (along with dogs, cats, and a horse) in God's country, the bluegrass of Kentucky. Her life's vocation has been to tell the stories that connect people and communities, first as a journalist, then as a diocesan communicator, and now through her ministry with Forward Movement. She is active in her church, St. Andrew's in Fort Thomas, and loves to spend time camping, playing games, and trading tales (and s'mores) around the fire. *Pages 139, 174, 191*

Winnie Varghese serves on the staff of Trinity Church Wall Street. She joined the staff at Trinity in 2015. Prior to that, she served as the rector of St. Mark's in the Bowery and as the Episcopal chaplain at Columbia University. Winnie is interested in the implications of the gospels for our common life. *Page 44*

Marek P. Zabriskie is the tenth rector of Christ Church in Greenwich, Connecticut, a thriving, 270-year-old congregation that is becoming increasingly Bible-centered and inspired in its ministries. He has served congregations in Nashville, Tennessee; Richmond, Virginia; and Fort Washington, Pennsylvania. He founded The Bible

Challenge and the Center for Biblical Studies to promote it globally in 2011. More than a million people have used The Bible Challenge to read through the entire Bible in a year. *Pages 40, 59, 157*

The Way of Love

Ministries that Live Out The Way of Love

We asked contributors to share ministries that embrace the practices of the Way of Love. As you learn about these ministries, you may feel inspired to support them with your gifts of time or treasure—or to seek out a similar ministry (or start one) in your local community. Put those practices into practice!

DIANA DOROTHEA DONCASTER, CT: The service to which I am currently called is primarily in worship and prayer and the solitary activities of writing, handcrafting, liturgy, and music. I am also privileged to serve as a spiritual director and retreat leader. I was duly humbled to be named The Official Hymn-Writer in Residence for Forward Movement's annual Lent Madness (www. lentmadness.org). The Community of the Transfiguration, in which I am a Sister and priest, runs Bethany School for kindergarten through eighth grade, St. Monica's Recreation Center, and the Transfiguration Spirituality Center, along with individual ministries. Learn more: www.ctsisters.org.

JENIFER GAMBER: The Society of the Companions of the Holy Cross (SCHC) is an intentional community of more than 800 women committed to a life of simplicity, thanksgiving, and intercession. Begun by Emily Morgan and shaped in its early life by the life and work of Vida Scudder, the SCHC is committed to justice and peace, the unity of God's people, and the mission of God in the world. The Companionship welcomes women in the Episcopal Church and other churches with whom the Episcopal Church is in communion. Learn more: www.adelynrood.org

JERUSALEM GREER: I lead and host a biweekly small group for my local parish at our family's hobby farm. We meet every other Sunday evening for food, fellowship, and formation. We are an intergenerational group, and because of this our gatherings are punctuated by kids dancing, singing, playing, laughing, and crying, which makes the whole experience feel like a family reunion at every meeting. Together we celebrate the liturgical year and the seasons of life. Our time together is generally focused around one of the Way of Love practices, and together we are digging in to what it means to live, move, and have our being in Christ.

BRENDA HUSSON: I serve on the advisory board of RenewalWorks. I have found their work an extraordinary gift in assessing the spiritual vitality of my parish and helping us discover the ways in which we could and now are growing in discipleship. It has been the ideal partner for us and our commitment to the Jesus Movement and Christ's way of love. Learn more: www.renewalworks.org

ROGER HUTCHISON: Using art and books as tools, I started The Painting Table, with a mission to reach out to hurting communities, both near and far. Whether sharing books with others or talking about color, art, and grief, I strive to live a life that tells a cohesive story, one of intentional, empathetic outreach. This was born through my experience with writing *The Painting Table* and offering Painting Table workshops. There is a subtle rhythm to what happens when people gather around The Painting Table. Participants are often guarded, and I sense a palpable fear in the air...the familiar one of "I'm not 'good' enough. I'm not an artist." Participants will sit for a moment staring at the blank paper. They ask me what they should paint. I encourage them to tell their own story using color, not words.

Gathering around The Painting Table is eucharistic in nature. There is a connection to something deeper. It is a glimpse into our souls. For some, the experience can only be described as holy. People begin to relax, and for many, it is the first time they have relaxed in days or weeks. Oftentimes there are tears. There are always gentle smiles. People are desperate for community. We live in a world where fear of the "other" threatens to take hold. We can't let that happen.

SHANNON MACVEAN-BROWN: I serve as president of Faith in Indiana, a multi-faith, multi-ethnic (really multi-everything) organization creating racial and economic equity for families in Indiana. Our diverse group proposes innovative solutions to address problems faced by rural, suburban, and urban families across the state. We have worked with community stakeholders to find community-based solutions to issues such as transportation, criminal justice reform, and immigration. We believe that since God is a God of love, there should be opportunities for all! As people of faith, we set audacious goals because we trust the grace of God that has brought us together. I've been so blessed to see people find their voice and take leadership in our communities. All that we do together is grounded in prayer and reflection. Our work brings about spiritual and community transformation. Learn more: www.faithinindiana.org

ANDREW MCGOWAN: I lead a community of formation for clergy and lay leaders for the Episcopal Church and the Anglican Communion within Yale University. Berkeley's students are training to minister in leading parishes, unconventional settings, and to be thought leaders for the Church as it faces a challenging future. Learn more: www. berkeleydivinity.yale.edu

SANDRA T. MONTES: The Episcopal Church Foundation Vital Practices has many resources for church leaders on topics like stewardship, discipleship, and evangelism. We also create original resources in Spanish by Latino/Hispanic leaders in the Episcopal Church. Through a Lilly Endowment grant we are able to fund Spanish-language financial literacy events to help our Latino/Hispanic leaders learn how to be financially knowledgeable with personal and church finances. Learn more: www.ecfvp.org

MARY FOSTER PARMER: Invite Welcome Connect is a ministry of transformation that equips and empowers individuals and congregations to cultivate intentional practices of evangelism, hospitality, and belonging. Rooted in the gospel directive to "Go and make disciples of all nations" (Matthew 28:19), the vision of Invite Welcome Connect is to change the culture of the Episcopal Church to move from maintenance to mission. Learn more: www.invitewelcomeconnect.sewanee.edu

C. K. ROBERTSON: As canon to the presiding bishop, I have the privilege of working with a remarkable group of directors and staff in four departments who day in and day out help build bridges beyond ourselves and live out the Way of Love on both a national and global level on behalf of countless Episcopalians. It is easy to look at the divisions and struggles in our nation and world, and yes, even in the Church and Communion. But as vital parts of the Episcopal branch of the Jesus Movement, these departments—Global Partnerships, Ecumenical & Interreligious Relations, the Washington, D.C.-based Office of Government Relations, and Episcopal Migration Ministries—have been conduits by which our church quite literally saves lives, feeds the hungry, welcomes the refugee, advocates for the voiceless, and in ways more numerous than I can count makes a difference in Jesus' name. Learn more: www.episcopalchurch.org.

CHRISTOPHER SIKKEMA: I have found a calling from God in learning and telling the stories of the Church, especially through the web series *Traveling the Way of Love,* dedicated to highlighting life-changing ministries and practices. Learn more: www.episcopalchurch.org/traveling-the-way-love.

DANIEL SIMONS: I am working to bring the Trinity Retreat Center back online as an incubator for a "spiritual ecology" for our time. Through retreats, workshops, and partnerships the center fosters circles of spiritual practice, builds leadership around creation care, and increases participants' capacity to build the beloved community. Learn more: www.trinityretreatcenter.org

BECCA STEVENS: Thistle Farms is a nonprofit social enterprise based in Nashville, Tennessee, dedicated to helping women survivors recover and heal from prostitution, trafficking, and addiction. We provide a safe place to live, a meaningful job, and a lifelong sisterhood of support because we believe love is the most powerful force in the world. Learn more: www.thistlefarms.org

RICHELLE THOMPSON: At Forward Movement, we gather every morning for prayer, reading the reflection from *Forward Day by Day* and sharing the prayer requests from our online community. While much of our work is the nuts and bolts of writing and publishing, we strive to never lose sight of our mission to inspire disciples and empower evangelists. We are not a publishing house. We are a ministry. That means we give away some of our resources to hospitals and prisons, Navy ships and river barges. We try to listen for and respond to the needs of the wider church, and we actively seek ways in which our ministry can support individuals and congregations in embracing the spiritual practices of the Way of Love. Learn more: www.ForwardMovement.org

WINNIE VARGHESE: At Trinity Wall Street, we do everything together; there is always a team behind any effort we make. I am proud to be a part of those teams and proud of what we accomplish together. Right now, I am moved by the work we are doing to highlight the plight of people trapped in our bail system—people who for lack of money wait in jail for a court date. These are stories most of us would never know except when something horrific happens, like a pre-trial death. Trinity's work on these issues and with these affected communities has brought the terror of the threat of being trapped in jail home for all of us. I cannot be at peace with so many of our neighbors living under this real threat daily. We will work together for change. Learn more: www.trinitywallstreet.org

MAREK P. ZABRISKIE: I encourage readers to explore The Bible Challenge and its many resources. The goal of the Center for Biblical Studies is to help as many people as possible develop a lifelong daily spiritual discipline of prayerfully reading the Bible in order to transform every day for the rest of their lives. No spiritual practice better equips Christians as disciples than daily engagement with scripture. The Bible Challenge produces a more committed, articulate, and contagious Christian, which in turn can create a more dynamic church in the Lord's service. Learn more: www.thecenterforbiblicalstudies.org

About Forward Movement

Forward Movement is committed to inspiring disciples and empowering evangelists. We live out our ministry through publishing books, daily reflections, studies for small groups, and online resources. More than a half-million people read our daily devotions through *Forward Day by Day*, which is also available in Spanish (*Adelante Día a Día*) and Braille, online, as a podcast, and as an app for your smartphones or tablets. We actively seek partners across the church and look for ways to provide resources that inspire and challenge. A ministry of the Episcopal Church since 1935, Forward Movement is a nonprofit organization funded by sales of resources and gifts from generous donors. To learn more, visit www.ForwardMovement.org.